TWAYNE'S WORLD AUTHORS SERIES

A Survey of the World's Literature

Sylvia E. Bowman, Indiana University
GENERAL EDITOR

AUSTRALIA

Joseph Jones, University of Texas
EDITOR

Christina Stead

(TWAS 95)

TWAYNE'S WORLD AUTHORS SERIES (TWAS)

The purpose of TWAS is to survey the major writers —novelists, dramatists, historians, poets, philosophers, and critics—of the nations of the world. Among the national literatures covered are those of Australia, Canada, China, Eastern Europe, France, Germany, Greece, India, Italy, Japan, Latin America, New Zealand, Poland, Russia, Scandinavia, Spain, and the African nations, as well as Hebrew, Yiddish, and Latin Classical literatures. This survey is complemented by Twayne's United States Authors Series and English Authors Series.

The intent of each volume in these series is to present a critical analytical study of the works of the writer; to include biographical and historical material that may be necessary for understanding, appreciation, and critical appraisal of the writer; and to present all material in clear, concise English—but not to vitiate the scholarly content of the work by doing so.

Christina Stead

By R. G. GEERING

University of New South Wales

Twayne Publishers, Inc.   ::   New York

For Dorothy

Preface

THE most comprehensive study of its kind to date, H. M. Green's *A History of Australian Literature*, deals with only three of Christina Stead's books, because Green found it necessary to restrict himself to writers working in Australia and to books whose material is obviously Australian. He believes Christina Stead is one of Australia's leading novelists and he writes enthusiastically, and at some length, about *Seven Poor Men of Sydney*. Apart from this, Green still manages to do less than justice to his particular subject. Since only a few of the stories in *The Salzburg Tales* have Australian settings, one paragraph of general comment is perhaps all that can be expected on that book. But Green's treatment of *For Love Alone* is surprisingly skimpy and unsympathetic; furthermore, he says that after *House of All Nations* Christina Stead's talent fades—a most questionable assertion, which the limitations he has placed on material for inclusion in his *History* will not allow him the opportunity of demonstrating.

Other critics have passed over a large area of Christina Stead's fiction, not for reasons as understandable as Green's but, apparently, on the assumption that because it does not treat Australian subjects it is rootless and therefore not worth considering. Certainly Christina Stead's work as a whole has received less attention from her compatriots than it deserves. Whatever the reasons, the fact remains that Australian critics have repeatedly overlooked a novel of the stature of *The Man Who Loved Children*, which was widely and warmly acclaimed on its recent republication in both England and the United States.

In this, the first full-length study of her work yet to appear, Christina Stead is approached as a novelist who happens to have been born in Australia, but who has something valuable to say to readers of literature in the English tongue everywhere. This is not to deny the significance of her Australian birth and upbringing; it *is* to insist that she is, in the best senses of the terms, sophisticated and cosmopolitan. The scope of her work is one indication of this —it ranges from fantasy to realistic documentation; it moves through the layers of class and from one continent to another; it is marked by intellectual curiosity and speculation, a poetic use of language, satiric observation, and an imaginative entry into character. Qualities such as these are not the preserve of any one country and it is on them that this study concentrates.

As pointed out in the Introduction, some of Christina Stead's earlier books, in addition to *The Man Who Loved Children,* have recently been republished. Two of the best that remain out of print (and, incidentally, two quite different kinds of novels) are *House of All Nations* and *The People with the Dogs;* I have, consequently, quoted rather more freely from them than from the others in order to give the reader an idea of their very individual flavors. Since this is a first study and since some of the books are still scarce, a certain amount of basic exposition has been necessary. Accordingly, I have provided a summary of the plot and indicated the central concerns of each novel before proceeding to criticism. It has not been possible to treat *Dark Places of the Heart* as fully as the other books. It appeared after the various proportions of this study had been established and all but the final chapter written. I have treated it sparingly, because of space limitations, in Chapter 6, where the reader will find a fairly brief discussion of its theme and setting, its heroine, and its relationship to other parts of Christina Stead's work. *The Salzburg Tales,* obviously, could not be summarized in the same way as the novels; so in dealing with it I have had to rely more on general descriptive comments and (by way of support) on an analysis of a few of the best and most representative of the stories.

The prime task of such a study as this I take to be the positive appreciation of the writer's work. This is usually more difficult to bring off than the persistent fault-finding that sometimes passes for literary criticism. Much of our current criticism, it seems to me, simply provides the critic with opportunities for establishing his superiority over the artist whose work he is taking apart. I am not suggesting the critic abdicate his responsibilities—if he finds faults he should point them out; but true judgment involves positive evaluation as well. Furthermore, one can read many a modern commentary without ever feeling that the critic liked what he read or sought to communicate a sense of enjoyment to his readers. I have tried throughout this study to lay emphasis on what is valuable and enjoyable in Christina Stead's work.

I wish to thank the following for providing material that has been drawn upon in the writing of this book: Miss Gwen Walker-Smith, Mr. and Mrs. Walter Stone, and Mr. David Stead, all of Sydney. My deepest thanks go to Christina Stead herself, who has allowed me access to her files and unpublished manuscripts. I have called upon her for information and help many times over the last six years without ever exhausting her courtesy, kindness, and generosity. I wish to put on record here the great debt of gratitude I owe her.

I should like also to express my thanks to the University of New South Wales for granting me the sabbatical leave during which this book was written.

R. G. GEERING

University of New South Wales
Kensington
Australia

Acknowledgments

The author is grateful to the following for permission to quote from copyright: Christina Stead for extracts from *The Salzburg Tales, House of All Nations, A Little Tea, a Little Chat,* and *The People with the Dogs;* Angus and Robertson, Ltd., for extracts from *Seven Poor Men of Sydney* and *For Love Alone;* Holt, Rinehart and Winston, Inc., and Martin Secker and Warburg, Ltd., for extracts from *The Man Who Loved Children.*

Contents

Chronology

1902 Christina Ellen Stead born July 17, in Rockdale, N.S.W., Australia, only child of David Stead and Ellen Stead (née Butters).

1904 Family moves to Oakleigh Villa, Rockdale. Mother dies.

1907 Father marries Ada Gibbons. Family moves to Lydham Hall, Bexley.

1914 Christina attends Kogarah Intermediate High School.

1915– Attends St. George's High School.
1916

1917 Family, now seven children in all, moves to Watson's Bay, just inside the South Head of Sydney Harbour.
Christina becomes a pupil at Sydney High School where she edits, and contributes prose and verse to the school magazine, *The Chronicle*.

1919 Begins two year course of training at Sydney Teachers College. Edits college magazine for two years.

1921 Awarded scholarship and becomes Demonstrator in Experimental Psychology at College.

1922 Starts teaching but suffers voice strain and transfers to Correspondence School of N.S.W. Department of Education.

1923 Returns to Teachers College and undertakes psychological testing in schools.

1924 Takes up another teaching appointment. Further voice trouble; leaves Department of Education.

1925 Learns typing and shorthand and takes up clerical work.

1928 Leaves Sydney, March 28, by the "Oronsay" for London. Gets a job with a firm of grain merchants in the City. Begins writing *Seven Poor Men of Sydney*.

1929 Goes to Paris to work in a bank in the Rue de la Paix.

1931 Visits Salzburg for Festival.

1934   *The Salzburg Tales* published in January, *Seven Poor Men of Sydney* in October, both in London. Short story, "O, If I Could but Shiver," included in anthology *The Fairies Return.*

1935   Gives up job in Paris bank and returns to London. Attends First International Congress of Writers for the Defense of Culture, June 21–25, and writes report for *Left Review,* August. Pays first visit to United States.

1936   *The Beauties and Furies* published in London. In Spain at outbreak of Spanish Civil War, leaves San Sebastian and crosses border into France.

1937   Finishes *House of All Nations* in Montpellier. Makes second visit to United States and settles there.

1938   *House of All Nations* published in New York.

1940   *The Man Who Loved Children* published in New York.

1943   Senior Writer with M.G.M., Hollywood. Conducts course, "Workshop in the Novel," at New York University, 1943–44.

1944   *For Love Alone* published in New York.

1945   *Modern Women in Love,* New York, an anthology of twentieth-century fiction, edited by Christina Stead and William Blake.

1946   *Letty Fox: Her Luck* published in New York. Leaves United States for Antwerp.

1947   Arrives in Antwerp. For the next four years lives in various places on the Continent—Antwerp, Montreux, Bologna, Basle, Brussels, Lausanne—and for a period, 1949–50, in London.

1948   *A Little Tea, a Little Chat* published in New York.

1951   Back in Paris again.

1952   Goes to live in The Hague. *The People with the Dogs* published in Boston. "The Hotel-keeper's Story" published in *Southerly,* Sydney.

1953   Settles in England.

1955   *Great Stories of the South Sea Islands,* selected, with a Foreword by Christina Stead. Translation from the French of *Colour of Asia* by Fernand Gigon.

1956   Translation from the French of *The Candid Killer* by Jean Giltène and *In Balloon and Bathyscaphe* by Auguste Piccard.

Chronology

CHAPTER 1

"Far other worlds, and other seas"

T HERE are welcome signs that Christina Stead, one of the few important Australian novelists, is coming back to favor after a period of comparative neglect. The recent Holt, Rinehart, and Winston edition of *The Man Who Loved Children* has made a strong impression in the United States, and Australian readers are now able to obtain *Seven Poor Men of Sydney, The Salzburg Tales,* and *For Love Alone,* all of which have long been out of print. Further interest will be aroused, too, by the publication soon of new works, the first books by Christina Stead to appear since *The People with the Dogs,* 1952.

I   *Literary Reputations*

Literary reputation is a fickle thing, especially in the contemporary scene. A skillful novelist with an eye for the topical and controversial is always likely to be overpraised, while genuine original talent goes largely unrecognized by the general reading public. Morris West is far better known than Christina Stead. Among more sophisticated and critical readers there may develop different kinds of approval, which are misleading because of their restrictiveness. Professional critics, like ordinary lending-library readers (but perhaps less often) are subject to fashions, and admiration for a certain writer can generate unspoken assumptions about the one kind of novel that deserves the epithet "great." To judge from some Australian critics it might be thought that Patrick White is the only Australian novelist worth bothering about today. Criticism of his work has become the major Australian literary industry and continues to grow. This, in some ways, is unfortunate. One effect of it is to overlook earlier and equally original contributions to Australian fiction; another is to ignore contemporary writers who may still deserve attention.

Christina Stead's work began to appear in the early 1930's, but

it was not until 1965 that a book of hers was published in Australia. (In passing it might be noted that many of the leading Australian novelists have been published mainly, or entirely, overseas.)
Over a period of more than thirty years she has devoted much of
her life to writing and has produced eleven books, all of them
written outside her native land. She left Australia in 1928 and has
never returned, and this is one reason why her work is less well
known in her homeland than it should be. Furthermore, her early
fiction, sophisticated, yet often passionate and strangely colored by
fantasy, though praised by well-qualified judges, was not likely to
appeal to those of her fellow countrymen reared largely on naturalistic novels dealing with such traditional Australian topics as
the convict past and life in the outback. Like a number of important Australian artists Christina Stead has always had strong ties
with Europe but the relationship, as we shall see later in this
chapter, is not simply that of the expatriate. There is no self-conscious striving after alien gods; she is to be thought of, rather,
along with such writers as Christopher Brennan, Henry Handel
Richardson, Martin Boyd, and A. D. Hope (to mention a few
sufficiently diverse talents), whose work takes its place, as a matter of course, within the general framework of European literature.

II *Early Life*

Christina Ellen Stead, eldest child of David Stead, eminent
Australian naturalist, was born on July 17, 1902, at Rockdale, one
of the southern suburbs of Sydney, New South Wales. Her father
remarried some years after the death of his first wife and Christina grew up at Bexley (near Rockdale) and, from 1917 onward,
at Watson's Bay, by the entrance to Sydney Harbour, in a younger
family of four half-brothers and two half-sisters. The former family home has been described by a cousin: "There was a marine
museum of rare specimens; reptiles coiled sleepily in the snake-
house; guinea pigs cropped the lawns under moveable frames;
there were lizards, an opposum and a tame kookaburra. A ram-
bling old place on a hill at Bexley, 'Lydham Hall' was an ideal
home for an imaginative child. Extensive grounds were sur-
rounded by a belt of ancient pine trees, and there was an orchard
and paddocks, where tall grasses grew undisturbed." [1] Watson's
Bay is the Fisherman's Bay so powerfully described in her first

novel, *Seven Poor Men of Sydney,* and appears again as the locale for the Hawkins home in "The Island Continent," the first half of *For Love Alone.*

Christina displayed literary gifts from an early age; she was a great reader and storyteller as a child, at thirteen she began to learn French and soon became an admirer of Guy de Maupassant, and while a pupil at Sydney High School she edited the school magazine. She trained at Sydney Teachers College and after completing her course became a demonstrator in psychology. For two years she edited the college magazine. Her first books, *The Salzburg Tales* and *Seven Poor Men of Sydney,* confirm by implication what is known from biographical sources of the range of her interests and reading in these early years. Behind *The Salzburg Tales* can be felt the whole fascinating world of European folklore and legend (congenial to a young writer with a decided bent for the fantastic and the grotesque), *The Arabian Nights,* Boccaccio, and Rabelais; behind *Seven Poor Men of Sydney* the writings of Poe, Nietzsche and the twentieth-century psychologists and social reformers. But long before these two books were written she had resolved to travel and work overseas; to this end she found employment in an office and set about the painful task of accumulating the money for her fare, at the same time attending a business class at night to equip herself for secretarial work. A young woman's determination to seek her future overseas, the desire for freedom, and the sense of a destiny (as yet ill defined) are among the experiences vividly realized many years later in the story of the courageous Teresa, the heroine of *For Love Alone.*

III   *Europe. The First Books*

The late 1920's saw the beginning of the great depression— hardly the most favorable time for a young woman to travel on her own from Australia to England and start looking for work in a strange land. As it happened Christina Stead was fortunate enough to find a job with a firm of grain merchants soon after she arrived in London. In 1929 she obtained secretarial work with a bank in Paris; she stayed with this bank for over five years and travelled between Paris and London on many confidential missions. The first hand knowledge she gained then of the world of European finance provided material she was later to draw on for *House of All Nations.* This, the longest, and in some ways the

most ambitious of all her novels, did not appear till 1938. The first
two books grew out of her earlier experience. *Seven Poor Men of
Sydney*, like many first novels, explores the passions and crises of
early adult life. It is obviously not an autobiographical novel as is
Lawrence's *Sons and Lovers;* the basic material, it seems, has un-
dergone a freer handling than Lawrence's but both in its uninhib-
ited choice of subjects and in its unashamedly intense treatment
Seven Poor Men of Sydney is comparable to *Sons and Lovers. The
Salzburg Tales* is quite a different sort of book. It takes its origin,
ostensibly, from a visit Christina Stead made to the Salzburg Festival in 1931 but its real roots go deeper into the past. A reader
knowing nothing of the author would be most likely to assume on
the evidence of this book that she was English with a long association with the life and culture of the Continent. The imaginative
foundation of these tales is literary rather than personal (which is
not to discount the contribution of her early reading to personal
experience), and it is this which gives the book a different flavor
from that of *Seven Poor Men of Sydney.*

Christina Stead's first novel is her only book set entirely in Australia. *For Love Alone* takes its heroine to England in the second
half of the book. Apart, then, from one and a half novels and a
few stories with Australian settings among the many that
constitute *The Salzburg Tales,* Christina Stead's work has nothing
distinctively Australian about it. It is, however, beside the point to
complain, as some Australian critics have done, that Christina
Stead is lost as a writer because she has left her native land and
has failed to continue writing about it from the other side of the
world. This view invites the rejoinder that simple national prescriptions (indeed rigid prescriptions of any kind) do not apply to
the creative artist; the writer must take his subjects when and
where he finds them and do the best he can with them, or he must
hope that the right subject has chosen him. The country and the
kind of society in which a novelist spends his early years will obviously affect the book he writes—he might glory in them, or he
might reject them. Neither response automatically guarantees a
good book, or a bad one. Self-conscious nationalism favors critical
clichés about the discovery of origins, and planting roots in native
soil. More often than not this kind of pronouncement is merely the
expression of a critic's desire for an American/English/Australian

novelist to write a recognizably American/English/Australian novel—a simple and sometimes a dangerous formula.

Christina Stead's novels, obviously (and naturally) enough, have grown out of the rather roving life she has led. She has always been interested in France and in French literature and it is not surprising that her third book, *The Beauties and Furies* (1936), is a novel of student life and love, set in Paris. *The Beauties and Furies* is not, in fact, a successful novel, but the reasons for its failure, as we shall see later, are not that it is set in France instead of in Australia. *House of All Nations,* a book of great scope and power is on another level altogether; it seems, almost, the work of a different writer, even though it too is set in Paris. Completed in France in 1937 it marks the end of the first phase of Christina Stead's literary career. In 1935 she had paid her first visit to the United States; the Civil War forced her out of Spain in 1936 and after some moving about in Europe she went again to the United States in 1937, where she stayed until the end of World War II.

IV *The United States*

All the novels written in or about this period, with the exception of *For Love Alone* (1944), have American settings: *The Man Who Loved Children* (1940), *Letty Fox: Her Luck,* hereafter referred to as *Letty Fox* (1946), *A Little Tea, a Little Chat* (1948), and *The People with the Dogs* (1952). *The Man Who Loved Children* has often been acclaimed her masterpiece and it is, indeed, a splendid book, which along with *For Love Alone* marks the peak of her achievement to date. These two are, I believe, among that select group of first-class novels so far produced by Australian writers and will surely become more widely appreciated now that they have been reprinted. They have a controlled intensity of vision that makes most Australian fiction look decidedly dull and anaemic. The other three books of this period, though variable in quality, all show Christina Stead's absorbed interest in different manifestations of American life: *Letty Fox* deals with the frantic search for female freedom in American middle-class society of the 1930's and 1940's. *A Little Tea, a Little Chat,* through its study of Robbie Grant, a bewildered libertine, depicts too the shady side of the New York business world. *The*

People with the Dogs, the mellowest of all Christina Stead's books, breaks new ground and looks into an area of American life inhabited by feckless and rather charming descendants of nine-teenth-century European liberals, a segment rarely explored by novelists of the social scene.

Like many good novelists Christina Stead is fascinated by man as an individual and man as a social being. *Seven Poor Men of Sydney* and *The Beauties and Furies* tend to stress the personal and the idiosyncratic, to present individuals at odds with society, which implies, of course, both the pressure and the inertia of custom and environment. The books from *House of All Nations* onward exhibit a closer social documentation and give more at-tention to the family unit, the larger and looser groupings of a person's friends and acquaintances, and the more impersonal worlds of business and politics. The novelist's desire to give detail and depth to the social picture while at the same time preserving the individuality of the key characters poses certain technical problems, as we shall see, in *House of All Nations* and *Letty Fox.*

As well as writing novels in the United States Christina Stead also worked for a short time in 1943 as Senior Writer with Metro Goldwyn Mayer in Hollywood, conducted a course, "Workshop in the Novel," for two terms at New York University 1943–44, and did literary criticisms for *New Masses* and the New York *Times.* She returned to Europe as soon as possible after the war travelling by cargo ship to Antwerp in December, 1946. Thereafter she lived in Switzerland, Italy, France and then (1952–53) in The Hague. She has since chosen permanent residence in England because, though fond of the Continent and fluent in several European lan-guages, she believes it best for a writer to be living with the lan-guage in which he is writing.[2] In England she has done some reviewing for the *Times Literary Supplement* and has continued writing fiction.

V *Expatriate Writers*

Like many Australians who have achieved eminence in the arts Christina Stead has left her own country to do so. When she first appeared on the literary scene in 1934 it was as a most unusual and promising young writer who had left her homeland six years before, settled abroad and found a London publisher. She had, in fact, offered a manuscript of a volume of short stories to an Australian firm for publication while she was still at Sydney Teachers College, but it was turned down and this experience must have strengthened her resolve to try her fortunes in England.

Many twentieth-century Australian novelists have felt the need of firsthand contact with European (or, at the very least, English) life and culture—Henry Handel Richardson, Helen Simpson, Martin Boyd, Patrick White are obvious examples; and even the more consciously nationalistic as well—Miles Franklin, Katharine Susannah Prichard, Vance Palmer. Ironically, the ardent patriots sometimes had to find their first publishers overseas.[3]

Expatriate writers do not, of course, run to a rigid pattern. The dramatist Ray Lawlor, who since the success of *Summer of the Seventeenth Doll* has himself spent most of his life abroad, points to one kind in the definition given by Alec in the play *The Piccadilly Bushman* (whose very title is significant): "the man who can never accept his own country and finds the country he hankers after never accepts him." This is the suspect kind, the restless, temperamental day-dreamer who just drifts and yearns. There is, next, the expatriate who, like Jack Lindsay, leaves his homeland to look for things he believes are essential to him, things that his own country will not or cannot provide. There is, finally, the kind identified by R. P. Blackmur in which physical expatriation only furnishes the external drama necessary to bring out the value of individual experience, the kind typified by James and Eliot, which (according to Blackmur's argument) poses a relationship that may bear rich artistic fruit—between outsider and insider, the unique and the representative, between the forces of anarchy and the forces of order.[4] Like all serious writers Christina Stead belongs to the second rather than the first of these groups; by temperament she is cosmopolitan not national in outlook and so she is, as it were, a natural expatriate. When she does deal specifically with the Anglo-Australian theme, the relationship of the Old World to the New, as in *For Love Alone*, she falls into Blackmur's category.

VI   The Old and the New Worlds

Strong as the attraction of Europe must have been to a young woman of Christina Stead's interests and ambitions it did not prevent her, as an artist, from seeing things there in her own way;

she has never abdicated her right to criticism. In her work there is
no simple rejection of Australia for Europe, no attempt to play off
a crude contrast between barbarism and culture. Henry Handel
Richardson took the phrase "Australia Felix," famous as a description of the rich lands discovered in western Victoria by Mitchell in
1836, and used it ironically as the title for the first volume of her
trilogy *The Fortunes of Richard Mahony*. There is no such irony
in Christina Stead's picture of life in twentieth-century Sydney.
The attention is focussed in *Seven Poor Men of Sydney* on the
struggles, the sufferings, and the spiritual plight of obscure folk,
and the setting might well have been any other poverty-stricken
city of the modern world. Australia, "felix" or "infelix," is not the
primary concern in either of the novels with Australian settings,
for in *For Love Alone*, again, the emphasis is individual and even
more intensified. It is a young girl's journey in search of love, and
love depends finally on persons not places. Christina Stead could
never be accused of flattering anything or anybody, and she certainly gives no pretty picture of Australian city and suburban life
in these two books; Teresa's revolt, to take but one example, guarantees the reader certain criticisms and rejections. However, she
looks at life just as sharply on the other side of the world: for
instance, Oliver, the vain and silly young Francophile in *The
Beauties and Furies*. *The Salzburg Tales* is rich in satiric observation and the massive *House of All Nations* is a savage indictment of European capitalism and high finance.

The attempt to find a satisfactory relationship between the New
World and the Old is one of the recurrent themes of Martin
Boyd's fiction. In an early novel of his, *The Montforts*, the problem is posed in terms of the extremes of barbarism and decadence.
In a later book the sense of expatriation is expressed thus in one of
the conversations between the married heroine and a middle-aged
admirer recently returned from abroad, once a childhood friend.

"You talk," said Diana, "not as if we *were* somewhere, but as if we
had to *go* somewhere. After all most people have to live in the coun-
tries where they're born, and they quite like it."
"Poor things," said Russell.
"Not at all."
"Well, let me think. I know that there's an answer to that. I've got it.
Only our bodies were born in Australia. Our minds were born in
Europe. Our bodies are always trying to return to our minds." [5]

Again and again Boyd's novels ring the changes on this theme but issues of this kind are not Christina Stead's basic concern, even though *For Love Alone* describes the heroine's escape from Australia to Europe. Boyd with all his love of Europe keeps coming back to Australia; Christina Stead having once made the break over forty years ago would, it seems, be content to go on writing about the life around her wherever she happens to be.

CHAPTER 2

Sydney and Salzburg

THE year 1934 saw the publication in London first of *The Salzburg Tales* and then of *Seven Poor Men of Sydney*. This has led some readers to assume, naturally enough, that *The Salzburg Tales* was the first book Christina Stead wrote. Colin Roderick even suggests that some of the tales form a prelude to *Seven Poor Men of Sydney* and that in them we may see the germs of her later work.[1] The truth is that *The Salzburg Tales* was written after *Seven Poor Men of Sydney* as, I believe, the more assured control of style implies. The facts are quite conclusive.

Reference was made in Chapter 1 to a manuscript of a volume of short stories which Christina Stead wrote while on the staff of the Sydney Teachers College. This manuscript, along with illustrations by an art teacher from the college, was submitted to the firm of Angus and Robertson, who were unwilling to publish. Not long after arriving in London Christina Stead became ill; she began to think she would not recover and it was then she started writing *Seven Poor Men of Sydney*, not with any thought of publication but because (to use her own words) she said to herself, "I am not just going to fade away, I am going to leave something." Later on Peter Davies saw the manuscript in Paris, was impressed by it and said he would publish it if she would give him another book first; so she sat down and wrote *The Salzburg Tales*. She had brought with her from Australia the manuscript for the earlier volume of short stories which had, in the meantime, been lost in Paris. *The Salzburg Tales*, her first published book, included four of the original stories, now rewritten, from the Australian manuscript; these were the only ones she could remember in detail—their Australian settings make them easy to identify: "The Triskelion," "Morpeth Tower," "On the Road," and "Day of Wrath."

I *The Australian Literary Background*

The first book then for consideration is *Seven Poor Men of Sydney* and to appreciate its significance it is necessary to look back beyond the 1930's. Australian literature is not much more than one hundred and fifty years old and its pattern of development and its dominant modes are reflections of that fact. In a newly settled country the struggle for survival and then for the basic physical comforts drains the energies of its people away from the arts. When a genuine local literature does begin to develop it will move away from its overseas sources toward new subjects and then, as artistic awareness increases, toward its own ways of expressing the national ethos. It was inevitable, and right, that Australian fiction from the later decades of the nineteenth century, by which time the move for federation was on its way, should concern itself with Australia's own story—with the convict past, the efforts of the early settlers, and the subsequent growth toward nationhood.

The nationalism of the 1880's and 1890's produced a vital and a parochial literature. Socially and culturally, as well as geographically, Australia remained remote from Europe up to World War I. Thereafter its isolation began to break down, but very slowly. The 1920's were the era of the *Vision* poets, who looked back and away from Australia for their inspiration, and of the Bohemians Jack Lindsay has written about in *The Roaring Twenties*. By the 1930's there was to be found an increasing awareness of English and of European literary traditions generally, which has grown immeasurably stronger in the last two decades. Even so, the fiction of the 1930's was still for the most part set in the older, conventional molds. Chester Cobb had experimented with the stream-of-consciousness technique in 1925 with *Mr. Moffatt*, but this was exceptional; so too was Robert Tate's *The Doughman* (1933), a strange, and in some respects a powerful allegorical story set against the realistic background of a Sydney bakery.

The best known and the most highly regarded Australian novelists writing just prior to 1934 were, probably, Miles Franklin, F. D. Davison, Vance Palmer, Katharine Prichard; Leonard Mann had at this time only one novel to his credit (*Flesh in Armour*, 1932). Brian Penton's *Landtakers* did not appear till 1934, and Kylie Tennant's *Tiburon*, till 1935. The first important book of

Eleanor Dark's was *Prelude to Christopher,* 1934. All of these writers were very much concerned with Australian subjects, mostly the outback or country life; none, with the exception of Eleanor Dark, showed any desire to experiment with the novel and try to extend its formal bounds. The general level of performance in fiction was sound in the 1930's and undoubtedly superior to that of the previous decade, but it could hardly be called venturesome. Apart from those already mentioned, three other novelists made original contributions to this decade, but not until toward the end—they were Kenneth Mackenzie with *The Young Desire It* in 1937, Xavier Herbert with *Capricornia* in 1938, and Patrick White with *Happy Valley* in 1939.

II   *Some Early Receptions of* Seven Poor Men of Sydney

Whatever comparisons are made, *Seven Poor Men of Sydney* was a most unusual sort of novel to appear on the Australian literary scene in 1934. It will be helpful to consider some of the typically unfavorable responses that Christina Stead's first novel has drawn from Australian readers—first from a professional reviewer in one of the leading daily papers, second from a practicing novelist of the traditional, nationalistic school. The *Sydney Morning Herald,* December 7, 1934, printed two unsigned reviews, one of Vance Palmer's *The Swayne Family,* prize winning novel in the Melbourne Centenary Competition, the other of *Seven Poor Men of Sydney.* A comparison of these reviews points to the literary assumptions the professional critic at that time was apt to bring to his task. (Whether or not the same critic reviewed both books does not matter now—both reviews clearly reflect similar attitudes and beliefs.)

The Swayne Family is not acclaimed as a masterpiece but is praised as a faithful chronicle, notable for its restraint, truth to life, sound craftsmanship, and impressive characterization. The critic approves mainly because the book displays the virtues of a competent and humane naturalism—we might infer that any book which moved outside this field of operation would be less sympathetically treated. It is interesting to note that he should find Palmer's picture of Melbourne so impressive for we shall see, later on, that one of the striking features of *Seven Poor Men of Sydney* is a vision of a city really notable for its imaginative power and its linking of scene and character to bring out the spiritual dilemmas explored. Palmer's critic is obviously won over too by the sort of characters the novelist draws—they are uncomplaining, they make the best of their abilities—in short they are worthy people. This all contributes to a highly favorable verdict. The reader today would probably endorse most of the descriptive remarks without attributing so much value to the inherent virtues of a chronicle and without finding the characterization outstanding. He might want to insist that *The Swayne Family* like many of Palmer's novels (the short stories are a different matter) is a book of safe, mild virtues, and a trifle dull.

In a reverse fashion the reviewer of *Seven Poor Men of Sydney* displays the same kinds of attitudes and criteria. He is unhappy because Christina Stead "avoids conventional methods of novel writing" and "leaves her readers to find their way through a maze of dialogue and descriptive matter as best they can." Having made this criticism he retracts it and falls into further confusion in the next sentence, where he says that though the result is "somewhat bewildering," the story "at least produces a more or less definite pattern, and the author's aim becomes reasonably apparent." And since the characters (unlike Palmer's) are not attractive and might all have fulfilled their function just as well in Teheran or Lima as in Sydney, the novel itself automatically goes down in his estimation. Yet (the same see-saw of statement and withdrawal goes on) the book cannot fail to impress . . . and the meaningless, ritualistic genuflections proceed. All of this reveals the critic's uncertainty when faced with something that does not conform to the conventional, naturalistic pattern, and the failure of his literary judgment when his moral bias toward the characters and his Australianism take over. To the literary establishment of the 1930's it was clear that *The Swayne Family* was a much better book than *Seven Poor Men of Sydney*. There are fewer readers today who would hold such a view.

Our second example comes from Miles Franklin's book on Australian writing, *Laughter, Not for a Cage*, which concerns particularly "the struggles, function and achievements of the novel in three half-centuries." [2] This book is an expansion of ten talks, eight of which were delivered as Commonwealth Literary Fund lectures in 1950 at the University of Western Australia. The date does not much matter; the general outlook is one that harks back to the self-applauding insularity and Australianism of earlier eras.

never satisfied unless spending herself in some idealistic pursuit,
works hard for the movement; Michael drifts along with them.

The focus shifts in Chapter 3 to Joseph Baguenault, Michael's
slow, good-natured cousin, and to Chamberlain's printing press.
Times are bad, salaries in arrears; Chamberlain is a waster and a
muddler, whose incompetence encourages Withers to scheme
against him and leaves him open to the designs of the shyster
Montague. Chapter 4 develops the picture of Joseph, a simple
orthodox Roman Catholic, and his relationship to the brilliant
young Jewish intellectual, Baruch Mendelssohn who, in his turn,
has come to depend on Joseph. This chapter also introduces the
seventh poor man, Tom Winter. Catherine now comes back into
the picture and Chapter 5 presents a long scene between her and
Mendelssohn in his slum dwelling by the city waterfront. From
this meeting we learn that she (as an earlier scene has already
suggested) loves Fulke and that Mendelssohn (though he brands
the Folliots pretty accurately as romantics and political dabblers)
is drawn to Marion. Withers, who acts as spokesman for the employees, is still in conflict with Chamberlain, and Mendelssohn
himself is planning to leave the country. Chapter 6 introduces Joseph to the fringes of the academic world, which is a mystery to
him. He listens to Winter, the Communist, inveighing against
church and state and goes with Baruch to a physics lecture at the
University, where for the moment he finds exhilaration in the new
world that seems to be opening up before him.

The story now comes back to Michael and Catherine again,
their conflicts, and Michael's increasing sense of isolation and unreality. Chapter 8 is the climax of the book; it describes Michael's
wanderings, a kind of lost spirit in search of his identity, first with
Withers and then by himself, and on through scenes of hallucina-
tions to his traumatic wartime experiences and his present hopeless love for Marion. After further wanderings he goes finally to
his death over the cliffs above his childhood home at Fisherman's
Bay. Michael's death shakes Joseph's religious trust and drives
Catherine to seek voluntary refuge in an asylum, teaching in a
workshop. Before she takes her leave of the world she tells Mendelssohn the strange story of Michael's past (as he once told it to
her) and admits that tormented unfulfilled love they had for each
other. By this time Chamberlain has gone bankrupt, the printers
have lost their jobs, and the economic depression has set in.

In the final chapter the group of friends, on the point of break-ing up, visits Catherine at the asylum. There they listen to the legend Kol Blount has composed in memory of Michael, a lost soul in a new-old continent; Catherine and Baruch make their farewells, she calmer now in the love that has grown for him and all his gentleness. The Folliots are due to return to England; Ba-ruch is to sail to a new job in America. Joseph, tranquil again, be-lieves he has come to know himself and can look to the future. The Endpiece is set some years later and shows Joseph walking home to his wife through a storm at the Bay to reflect upon the spiritual tempests long since past.

IV *A Poetic Novel about City Life*

Seven Poor Men of Sydney in concept and feeling is essentially a poetic novel and its loose structure is a consequence of this. It moves fairly freely in and around the lives of people related to one another in different degrees of intimacy. Some of them are thrown together by occupation, like Joseph and Mendelssohn, and others by family connection. Cutting across these are rela-tionships stemming from psychological and emotional needs such as those between Michael and the Folliots, and Michael and Kol Blount. Then again there are the links between people striving to make something of the social muddle around them—those seeking (some more genuinely than others) meaning in life through poli-tics (Winter and the Folliots), others through religion (the older Baguenaults and Joseph), others through the intellect (Mendels-sohn). Though they all experience frustrations of one kind or an-other, though they all sometimes feel at the mercy of forces, exter-nal or internal, beyond their control, they are not (despite Miles Franklin) "a gallery of ne'er-do-wells" or hopeless and passive neurotics—unless to be aware of the dilemmas of modern man and to feel deeply is to be neurotic. Michael is the only one who surrenders to the chaos within; Catherine drives herself to ex-haustion in idealist causes, Withers has the ruthlessness that in favorable circumstances could lead to success in business, Winter has the fanatic self-righteousness of the political activist, and Joseph displays the persistence and dependability of a good family man.[3]

This is a young writer's book about youth, its passions, and the frustrations of its ideals. It is, also, a book about poverty in a modern city and its effects upon human lives. Furthermore, whatever the intensification of the treatment and however fantastic the forms individual experience sometimes takes, it is (as the author claims) a book about humble (and basically even ordinary) people. This note is struck in the first chapter, when the Baguenault family is introduced:

There was a family there named Baguenault, which had settled in the bay directly after its arrival from Ireland thirty years before, and had its roots growing down into the soil and rocky substratum so that nothing seemed to be able to uproot it any more, so quiet, so circumspect in the narrow life of the humble, it lived; but disaster fell on it, and its inner life, unexpressed, incoherent, unplanned, like most lives, then became visible as a close and tangled web to the neighbours and to itself, to whom it had for so long remained unknown. Who can tell what minor passions running in the undergrowth of poor lives will burst out when a storm breaks on the unknown watershed? There is water in barren hills and when rain comes they spurt like fountains, where the water lies on impermeable rocks.[4]

Just before his death Michael, nursing his griefs, talks to Mendelssohn:

"What's concealed probably isn't worth telling."
"Don't say that," urged Baruch, "an insignificant thing may fill a man with passion. Lives wind their way out by curious bypaths. You may have noticed, official drama is so fearfully unsatisfactory because of its big gross themes. Everyone knows it doesn't represent their own feelings at all. There would be a row if real situations were reproduced; it would undermine the State. The State is built on grotesque comic-opera conventions which no one dares mock at." (p. 242)

This is the best statement from within of the kind of people and situations Christina Stead is writing about. Against Catherine's contempt for the tranquil and stupid Josephs of this world as uninteresting and beyond salvation must be placed Kol Blount's question: " 'What is as unfathomable as a simple man?' " (p. 62). Baruch, too, maintains that the Josephs have claims upon our love: " 'The quietest and simplest man can develop endlessly: even the lifelong sleeper can be awakened' " (p. 153). And, as if in proof of the proposition that the humble is not the commonplace, Joseph comes through better to the reader than some of the other, more flamboyant, characters.

As a story of city life, not life in the bush or the small country town, *Seven Poor Men of Sydney* is one of the exceptions among Australian novels of the 1930's. Australian fiction was slow to throw off its predominant concern with the bush as the source of all that was genuinely felt and distinctively Australian. *Seven Poor Men of Sydney* is a book which challenged such assumptions. It differed perhaps even more from most of the other fiction of its time by reason of its concentration upon the inner life in a poetic, expressionist way. This is not to overlook the author's sense of place; the city itself is vividly and often precisely described and this prevents the characters from becoming merely rarefied emotional states. The descriptions of Fisherman's Bay as Michael the growing lad knew it and the picture of the Woolloomooloo slums are fine examples of clear and evocative prose. Perhaps less noticeable at first reading are those more quietly toned passages, which through their description of place draw out implications for character at the same time. One such example comes from Chapter 4 where two of the poor men, Baruch and Joseph (with money in their pockets, the first time for weeks) go window-shopping—the wise man and the innocent, in simple enjoyment; nightfall finds them in a dowdy part of the city:

The lights were on dimly to light a little the interior dusk and still to admit what remained of the daylight; the street was not yet that covered way which is endless and mysterious at night, but the city had become warm, hospitable, a city of hearths and yellow-silk lighted interiors; spoons clapped on soup-plates, spoons clanked in cups, sugar-basins revolved. An old man out walking with a cane looked friendlily at the two boys, with the friendliness of a Biblical comment, "Look, what you are experiencing the prophets experienced in their adolescence two thousand years ago." He went stooping on. I am young, thinks Jo. This is what the old man intended him to think. The street-lights were switched on and glowed warmly in a slight thick dust, as if to prove conclusively that the day had knocked off work and gone home. Near an old garden, he noticed how the trees had taken on an inhuman air with something wild in them, as lions have, sitting unreconciled in the back of their cages licking their paws, in the zoo. He heard again the tapping behind him of the nocturnal prostitute just beginning her beat: fresh, odorous, with shining curls and a big bow on her neck and frilled elbows, pretty, dainty. She

smiled unconsciously as she tapped with vanity past him. More soft
steps and, rubbersoled, came the lamp-lighter who had just got
through the district of gas lamps. Tea was preparing everywhere;
night had begun.

"I am hungry," said Joseph.

Two old dowdy women huddling to each other, both thin, beaked,
satin-hatted, and hatpin-eyed, passed him and looked approvingly at
him because he was shabby, dull and modest. Joseph, too, felt com-
forted; his life had been passed amongst old shabby women. They
would do him no harm; they would make tea for him. (p. 122)

V *The Structure of* Seven Poor Men of Sydney
as Related to Character

This kind of treatment, linking scene and character, is intensified in those passages (as in Chapter 8) which express in natural
imagery the turbulence raging in Michael's mind. But, this being
said, what gives the apparently haphazard structure a unity of its
own is the deep conflict depicted between different views and
ways of life—this is the book's central, informing idea.[5] The
Times Literary Supplement missed this, as did most Australian
reviews. It will become increasingly clear in this study that one of
Christina Stead's most favored structural devices is the building
through contrasting characters and ideas.

Michael and Catherine are rebels, searching for ideals that are
unrealizable. They are both headed for defeat because they deny
too much. There is perhaps some future for Catherine as the book
ends, but for Michael none was possible. His is a fragmented personality which can never achieve completeness—his barely sup-
pressed incestuous love for Catherine is one manifestation of this
fatal disharmony. He once struggled to put this into words in his
confession to her: " '. . . and so I am in love with you; not you,
but that which is like you in me. I am lost because part of me is
sundered from me for ever.' " This curious self-analysis ends: " 'I
have no meaning in ordinary life, and this is what releases me
from being silent about my love, and it is what makes me love,
perhaps, the image of myself: it is a hunger and lust for death at
root' " (p. 274). The memory of this lies in Catherine's mind when
she says to Baruch, who has just expressed his love for Joseph,
the simple man: " 'I don't love him: patience, stupidity, irritates
me. He is part of the human scenery to me, as I said, of the same

stuff as the hills and as slow. Not like my brother Michael, a remarkable character, he. He does absolutely nothing, he is positively an abstract personality; he shows an inner struggle to union with himself and his counterparts; Michael eats his own flesh.'" To which Baruch replies: "'That is not unique. . . . They all develop this prodigious flowering of the sensibility and aimless intellection. Don't admire it; wish, rather, that he were like Joseph'" (p. 154).

Joseph represents the other extreme. Occasionally he is jolted out of his calm but never for long. He is the simple, good, unimaginative man, who can find solace in the family and the church. He accepts life, but at a cost. The madman's tale, "Disorder, Lord of the earth," strikes terror into the hearts of the other listeners, but it does not upset Joseph, who thinks to himself: "Here all these months have gone past and they are *still* talking a lingo that has no meaning to me. But why should I learn it? They are all throwing fits and I am calm, a dummy, but calm'" (p. 304). This recalls Baruch's words: "'. . . there's nothing so soothing to a brain storm as a contemplation of order in the universe'" (p. 240). Joseph's destiny is a safe, humdrum job, marriage and a tidy home at Fisherman's Bay, where he can shelter from the storms that blew Michael to his destruction.

Baruch Mendelssohn, intelligent, sensitive, and well-balanced, the most perceptive character in the book, stands between the yea and the nay-sayers. Baruch is not the infallible raisonneur, but of them all he is the most likely to speak truth. He understands Catherine, "a woman of revolution without a barricade" (p. 144), whose plight is represented in the symbolic painting he shows Joseph; his advice is practical and sympathetic; he tells her to get a real cause to fight for and not to be a prima donna, a dilettante heroine like Marion. When Catherine ends her talk with him by saying "'Michael *was* very strange: and only I know how strange. He was my *alter ego.*'", the scene concludes: "'You'll tell me all that some day,' said Baruch politely, examining her wild romantic, exaggerated pose" (p. 154). And he is proved right—Catherine does tell all in her narrative after Michael's death. The discerning reader will appreciate the force of the final phrase, which emphasizes both Mendelssohn's and the author's detachment from Catherine's emotional commitments.

VI *Imagery and Symbolism*

There are other features binding the various parts of the story together, notably certain images and symbols which recur like motifs. The first two chapters are rich in details that accumulate significance as the book grows: the Gap, a place notorious for suicides, is part of the physical environment in which Michael grows up and by Chapter 8 we realize how much a part it is of his mental landscape too; Michael's fear of and fascination with heights as a child are noted; then there is the flagstaff of the signal station: "It stretched up beyond its normal height into profound heavens where mists now bowled fast and dimly. In its mast and yards he saw the sign of his future, a monstrous pale tree, bitterly infinite, standing footless in the earth and headless in the heavens, a splinter sterile and sapless, a kind of scarecrow, a rack for cast vestments, a mast castaway: underneath the sea ran" (p. 40). This is perfect in its symbolic appropriateness to scene and character and is recalled as the brief, final touch when Michael goes to his death here years later. These early descriptions of cliff, wind, and sea often achieve the poetic power that landscape assumes in Hardy and the early Lawrence. It is as if Michael's boyhood spent here on the edge of the island continent looking out over the ocean somehow bespeaks the very precariousness of his hold on life.

The more pervasive imagery of the book is that of darkness and light, and it is in these terms that Michael attempts to explain his spiritual dilemma to Catherine. To Michael darkness and mystery seem to dominate the natural world, and darkness is the condition of man, though he always thirsts for the light. There is a rather obvious parallel to this in Joseph's temporary awakening to the nature of the universe after he has listened to the physics professor's lecture on light (Chapter 6). The prohibition on love between brother and sister Michael associates with the nameless dark mysteries. He goes on (and it is hard to follow him here): "'Whereas, as I was born unnatural, I have come to love my sister as myself, for you are myself, but everything appears in you with a greater perfection, and all that is dark and light in you is the very reflection of my own thoughts, my mind and my desires. A man cannot love himself, but all men do, and so there is no satisfaction in the world, for we must clasp another body, informed by another spirit to ourselves'" (p. 274). Michael, Catherine believes, wanted only to play with the idea of love between them, whereas for her it was all too real.

It is impossible to impose a tidy pattern upon the use of this imagery in the book as a whole; darkness, for instance, is associated by Kol Blount in Chapter 2 with the defiance of despair and then with love in general in a passage which, as we shall see later, anticipates in a quite remarkable way certain themes and relationships explored more systematically in *For Love Alone*. In the same section Blount, as if with preternatural foresight of Michael's death, talks of the three white nights before suicide, and we recall that the bewitching light of the moon has already been used (as it is to be used again later) as an accompaniment of phantasmagoric experiences.[6] Perhaps if she had continued writing novels like *Seven Poor Men of Sydney* Christina Stead would have employed this color symbolism on a larger scale, as Lawrence did in *The Rainbow* and *Women in Love*. At all events, there is a poetic logic in the description of Michael's end. As he stands on the cliff edge, "he is already no longer a man but part of the night." The sea claims him and "all through the early morning the strings of the giant mast cry out a melody, in triumph over the spirit lost" (p. 250).

Michael and Catherine seem to dominate the book though for long stretches they are not the obvious center of attention (rather like Heathcliff and Catherine I in *Wuthering Heights*) and, despite a certain theatricality, they are the most interesting characters. Michael's introspectiveness, the sudden leaps into fantasy, the sense of division and alienation are touched off perfectly again and again in the first two chapters—one thinks of White's *The Aunt's Story* as the next Australian novel comparable in this regard; "the ranges of human experience go beyond human belief" (p. 270). Of the other characters the best drawn are Withers, a strange Munchausen figure of a type that recurs in Marpurgo (*The Beauties and Furies*), and Joseph. Winter and the Folliots represent, mainly, political attitudes. Kol Blount is, even more, an emblematic figure; a life-long cripple, he is set apart and it is as a form of death-in-life that he attracts Michael. Blount says: " 'Michael is like me, paralysed, armless, a brother'" (p. 60).[7]

VII *Rhetorical Devices*

The poetic element in *Seven Poor Men of Sydney* accounts for most of its unusual features. In her attempts to plumb the emotional depths of her characters Christina Stead occasionally abandons naturalistic dialogue and casts their thoughts into a formalized poetic monologue. This kind of language is apt to get out of hand. Sometimes it lapses into the clichés of Romanticism, for example, " 'Because you are not beauty, you are terror, you are destiny, what is destiny but death, and what else are you? If I ever kissed you, what would I have under my lips but the very substance and moment of death and dissolution?' " (p. 274). At other times the rhetoric seems in excess of the scene's demands, as in one of Catherine's long speeches to Baruch (p. 149), or the young writer's fascination with words may run away with her, as in the free-associating catalogue of terms that occurs in Michael's account of one of his harrowing experiences (pp. 269–70).

Language used in a deliberately poetic way in novels always runs the risk of sounding queer. It is difficult for the reader to free himself of the naturalistic assumptions on which most novels for the greater part of their length depend; there is a barrier even with a book as great as *Moby Dick* when the transition from one level of language to another is made. In *Seven Poor Men of Sydney* the effect is melodramatic in scenes such as the last meeting between Catherine and Mendelssohn, where her stylized speech accompanies the ritualistic gesture with which she cuts her wrist. This kind of scene does not come off as well as that in which action is arrested and the rhetoric, highly mannered though it may be, is allowed to stand on its own, as for example, in the set-pieces delivered by Kol Blount.

A less obvious (and for that reason a more readily acceptable) form which the search for more intense expression may take is the rhetorical monologue, the long and highly articulate speech which, once again, goes beyond the bounds of ordinary language. This device occurs freely in Christina Stead's fiction; some of the characters in *House of All Nations* and *The Man Who Loved Children* are wonderfully eloquent and we know them so much better as a result. Baruch Mendelssohn of *Seven Poor Men of Sydney* is the first of these larger-than-life talkers, and even if his exuberance sometimes turns into displays of intellectual fireworks he is never dull. His voice seems closest to the author's; compare, for example, this from a long speech on poverty by Baruch to Joseph:

> "They tell you poverty keeps you from temptation; it certainly does: but what you need, my poor friend, is a little temptation. Items: pride, in belonging to a dominant class; covetousness, in respect of a new pair of pants; lust, enough to make an appointment with a pretty girl; wrath, when you find you're trod on; gluttony, for a beefsteak; envy, of the bounding health of rich children; sloth, the lying all day on a yellow beach staring into vacancy and getting brown. But the Church has cleansed your heart of the seven deadly sins for working men. You have pints of character, so much that you're scarcely fit for human conversation, Jo." (p. 89)

with the novelist's comment here:

> . . . in a voice which was intended as a trumpet call to the legions of light against Clod sitting in a quagmire, Prosy wrapped in cotton cocoon, and Tradition with fat hams sitting in his pew. (p. 144)

It is this kind of thing that leads Nettie Palmer, in an appreciative notice, to say: "To read her book is to spend your time in the company of an exhilarating author, who is probably a genius. But this is not enough: you have been living with the author, not with her characters." [8]

If used on a large scale any of the rhetorical devices described above tend to blur distinctions between characters. It is a question of how far the writer can afford (or is determined) to go in his search for heightened expression. He may be thoroughly systematic and elect to go the whole way to a supposedly logical conclusion, but who would claim that Virginia Woolf's *The Waves* is an unqualified success? Christina Stead herself has spoken revealingly on this subject in a discussion of *Seven Poor Men of Sydney*.

> "The Seven Poor Men" are not actually drawn from life; they are like most characters, crystallizations of various types of men and women; they do not express in their conversations my view of life, but, I hope (or rather intended) various views of life, according to their temperaments.
>
> Naturally, this is not always successful. Conversation is diffuse,

disjointed, full of popular sayings and banalities local in time and place which do not express character at all, or very little. My purpose, in making characters somewhat eloquent, is the expression of two psychological truths; first, that everyone has a wit superior to his everyday wit, when discussing his personal problems, and the most depressed housewife, for example, can talk like Medea about her troubles; second, that everyone, to a greater or lesser extent, is a fountain of passion, which is turned by circumstances of birth or upbringing into conventional channels—as, ambition, love, money-grubbing, politics, but which could be as well applied to other objects and with less waste of energy.

There are some whom this personal sentiment makes wanderers and some who stew all their lives in their own juice and ferment. I confess that the study of personality is a private passion, with me.[9]

As these comments imply, *Seven Poor Men of Sydney* springs from genuinely original impulses and personal conviction. It is not, despite certain critics, a consciously imitative book. It reflects, of course, some of the author's reading; we might recall Poe in Kol Blount's formal orations. We might think of *Gulliver's Travels* when we read:

There seemed to him to gleam above all this a city as on an adamant island, where the erudite lived and put the world to shame, told the truth to princes, and wrote tracts to enlighten the slaves. It is true, of course, that they write them to enlighten the poor, but they are usually sold at prices ranging from 10s.6d. to £2.2s., and the poor are too pig-headed to buy them. (p. 141)

Even so we must admit that Christina Stead has taken Swift's Laputan image and made of it something of her own. To take a broader example: Mendelssohn, talking to Catherine after Michael's suicide, remarks, " 'What an underground life was that!' " (p. 310). The reader, maybe, thinks of Dostoevsky's *Notes from Underground;* he then goes on to observe the parallels between the underground hero and Michael and concludes that Dostoevsky's book is an "influence" on *Seven Poor Men of Sydney*. In fact Christina Stead had not read *Notes from Underground* at the time of writing *Seven Poor Men of Sydney,* so the critic has to be content with noting certain similarities. Detecting influences is a favorite critical pastime but it can be a dangerous game; it is even more risky to talk of deliberate imitation when dealing with the work of a serious artist.

VIII   *The Salzburg Tales*

The *Times Literary Supplement* reviewer wrote of *The Salzburg Tales*: ". . . it is a pleasure to salute in her a story-teller of profuse imagination with a gift of ingenious and rollicking fantasy and a turn of language to match," and ends by saying ". . . it is difficult to decide which are the best of the stories. Their wide curiosity, their emotional detachment, their artistry and felicity of expression make Miss Stead a writer of unusual interest." [10] Few Australian writers have received such praise overseas for their first books. *The Salzburg Tales* is a more assured and sophisticated production than *Seven Poor Men of Sydney*, just as well, if not better, written, and, since it is a collection of stories, more difficult to describe in a few words.

Those who knew Christina Stead as a child recall her early skill in the spinning of tales; from the evidence of her writing it is clear that she has preserved her fondness for narrative, especially that leaning toward the bizarre. *The Salzburg Tales* is unmistakably the work of a writer whose imagination was continually fired by her reading of fairy tales, folklore and legend. Parts of *Seven Poor Men of Sydney* anticipate certain of the narrative veins that appear in *The Salzburg Tales*. There is the amusing tale of the stoker sent up from hell by the devil, so efficient that he stokes himself out of every job he takes and has finally to return to hell for full employment. Again, there are the strange visionary tales in Chapter 11, more like prose poems than ordinary stories. Both kinds find their parallels among the yarns that seem to flow effortlessly from the Centenarist in *The Salzburg Tales*. Other noteworthy instances outside this volume of stories are "O, If I Could But Shiver," a story included in *The Fairies Return*, a collection of parodies by various modern writers of traditional fairytales,[11] and the superb "Hawkins, the North Wind," told by Louisa to her younger brothers and sisters in *The Man Who Loved Children*.

IX   *The Plan of* The Salzburg Tales

Christina Stead has never surpassed the sheer brilliance of this early volume. It is a book in which the young writer seems to revel in the luxuriance of her special talents. *Seven Poor Men of*

Sydney looked inward; *The Salzburg Tales* is an outward-looking
book and reflects the buoyancy and confidence of the creative
spirit assured of the opportunity to express itself. It is a collection
of some forty stories (the number has to be approximate as the
Centenarist runs rather into streams of anecdotes and short fables
than to stories) set within a framework in the manner of *The
Decameron*. It consists of "The Prologue," a description of Salzburg at the August Festival; "The Personages," a description of
the people assembling for the open-air performance of the medieval play "Jedermann;" the tales themselves, spreading over seven
days; and "The Epilogue," after which "No-one can believe they
[the guests] listened another day." [12]

Every day some of the guests meet in the Capuchin Wood or in
the city itself and listen to tales as told by each of them in turn.
After listening to the first three stories the group appoints the Viennese Conductor as Master of Ceremonies. Each day is rounded
off by the Centenarist of whom it is said, "He was full of tales as
the poets of Persia: he unwound endlessly his fabrics, as from a
spool the silks of Arabia" (p. 38). Short interludes of description
and dialogue act as links between the stories. "The Personages"
lists forty people of whom thirty-one become narrators; it also describes bands of college girls and German youngsters who have
made their way to the festival. The general procedure is one story
from each narrator, though the Schoolgirl and the Old Lady both
tell two brief tales.

The forty or so pages comprising "The Personages" constitute a
delightful preface full of wit and vivacity. It would serve very
well to dispose of the criticism that Christina Stead is an imitative
writer. It does remind us of Chaucer's famous Prologue to *The
Canterbury Tales* but, in H. M. Green's words, it is an "elaborate
and sophisticated modern equivalent rather than an imitation." [13]
Original writing (or the best of it) does not exist outside literary
traditions; nor does awareness of the past mean simply imitation.
It is impossible to deny the highly individual flavor of the prose
here. The picture of the Viennese Conductor (probably the best
known of these vignettes) expresses a true, artistic delight in
touching off the poses and mannerisms of a histrionic musician—a
description which combines a zest for language with perfect literary control (pp. 12–13). Again and again the sparks fly, and they
do illuminate. The acuteness of observation is matched by a keen

wit and quick satiric thrusts. There is the middle-aged school-teacher, a serious scholar but naïve and given to good causes:

. . . her intricate, delicate and tenuous mind somehow transformed all she had learned into a kind of medieval manuscript with the modern instances as a cynical and even comic gloss. She said she believed in a Divinity not in God. Liberal, rationalist, philanthropist, she called herself, and she remained as foolishly credulous as a girl of fifteen: she had read all the white, blue, green, brown and yellow books published on crime, war, drugs, prostitution and atrocities, and she still believed in the sacredness of patriotic passion and the perspicacity of private interest. (p. 20)

There is the pretentious modern poet who "liked to rake through muck for a jewel" (p. 20), or the German philosophy student who "squirmed with delight at the sight of a little bit of tracery in a clerestory, and went into fits over the counterpoint of Brahms" (p. 27), or the rich but illiterate banker with a genius for making money: "If a king lay at death's door, he bought a bolt of crape, if a peasant girl in adolescent delirium saw the Virgin at her furrow's end, he started an omnibus line" (p. 39). Or, finally, the Critic of Music: ". . . he had a fine ear: he could hear a whisper in the farthest corner of a concert hall, and if he heard it he would frown tremendously: and he could hear the opinions of other critics three seats away, even in a tumult. He could hear the fluid in the tube of a barometer rising and falling and the rise and fall of the tides of opinion" (p. 45). The American critic Clifton Fadiman includes this prefatory material to *The Salzburg Tales* in his anthology *Reading I've Liked,* with this comment: "For wit, fancy, variety, light-brushwork satire, and almost offensive polish, these miniature novels are inimitable." [14]

H. M. Green says that "attitude and manner of telling do not vary so much as the characters of the tellers of the tales." [15] Nevertheless, Christina Stead makes some attempt to link the character as described with the kind of tale he or she tells. So the Broker, a lover of epithets and exotic literature, relates, "Don Juan in the Arena," a richly colored variation on the Don Juan theme, in which bull-fighting is linked with his amatory achievements and the Don goes to his death in the bull-ring. So the Police Commissioner, a shrewd and unscrupulous careerist, relates, "The Deacon of Rottenhill," a sardonic tale against the stupidity of authority, satirizing detectives and detective stories. The melancholy Danish Woman tells a supernatural tale of blighted love; and so on. I said "some attempt" because there are occasions where there seems no obvious connection or where a particular story appears most unlikely to have come from the narrator to whom it has been assigned. The allusive and sophisticated satiric play with legends in "Sappho" is certainly out of character for a young romantic schoolgirl. We might also have our doubts on this score about "Day of Wrath," "Antinoüs," "Silk-Shirt," and (one of the best stories in the volume) "In Doulcemer," though it could be argued that in the last two mentioned Christina Stead is indulging her own irony at the narrator's expense, thereby breaking the general structural pattern.

X Variety of Subjects and Moods

The tales exhibit an astonishing variety of subjects, characters, and moods; they vary greatly, too, in length and complexity from the curious scraps sometimes tossed out by the Centenarist, mingling history, superstition, and the supernatural, or the series of apostrophes and sketches in "Fair Women," to the elaborately patterned "The Gold Bride" and "The Mirror." There is, as has often been said, a strong element of fantasy in The Salzburg Tales but it is not the controlling force in all the stories and when it does appear it operates in a variety of ways and for a variety of purposes. Some of the stories are straightforward character studies done in a predominantly naturalistic manner, for example "Overcote," "Poor Anna"; others are recastings of legendary material, "Antinoüs," "A Colin, a Chloë"; some are frankly romantic tales, operatic in matter and manner, "To the Mountain," "The Gold Bride." As might be expected from a reading of "The Personages," satire is fairly frequent, most notably in "The Dean of Rottenhill," "In Doulcemer," and the Chekovian parody, "A Russian Heart." Apart from the Centenarist's stories there are others marked in varying degrees by the supernatural, for example "The Mirror" and "The Triskelion," with its disturbing picture of evil. Then there are those short pieces, anecdotes from which the narrator distils his moral, "The Sparrow in Love" and the simple but moving "The Death of the Bee." Fantasy colors a good many of the stories in addition to the supernatural and the romantic tales: it is present as subject in "Morpeth Tower," which relates a young girl's midnight imaginings; as subject again and as narrative device in "Silk-Shirt," the story of a successful architect bedevilled by fancies that always elude him; as a source of comedy in the Rabelaisian exaggeration of "Guest of the Redshields"; as a way of achieving the wryly ironic flavor in "Lemonias," and, finally, for satiric ends in the delightful "The Sensitive Goldfish." The irony that hovers so attractively over these last two stories occasionally takes on a bitter tone as in the more serious "The Amenities," which is the rare instance in this volume of a story that seems to go on for too long.

XI *Four Representative Stories*

A closer look at a few selected tales will give a better idea of their emotional range and provide a basis for some general observations. The first choice is "The Sensitive Goldfish," the story of an ambitious young securities clerk in the Bank of Central Honduras (London), whose job is to look after the 125 ancient and magical goldfish prized by the director Baron Franz—August de Geldreich. Whenever Henry (illegally) takes one of the fish home it finds its way back to the bank by the next morning. In the presence of a certain annual balance sheet one of the fish Henry has taken goes blood red, so he buys shares in this company and sells later at a handsome profit. Henry is able to sell one fish to ambitious clerks all over the city knowing it will always return of its own accord to the bank. One Friday, on the Jewish Day of Atonement when the Lord makes up all His accounts of good and evil for the year Henry, to his horror, finds all the goldfish dead and rotting in their tank. He takes his news hurriedly to the Baron, who is attending to his spiritual duties in the synagogue and who returns to cope with the crisis. On Monday the bank goes off the gold standard. Henry continues to do well with shares because, as a reward, the Baron has given him one pickled goldfish whose glowing and fading in the presence of certain information act as a guide to investment. The final sentence reads: "I should say that the rest of the goldfish have been secreted by the Baron, for they are not always exactly of the same shade of opinion, and he is then obliged to take a majority ruling" (pp. 261–62).

The details are all significant: Henry is a *securities* clerk, he invests in the *North Atlantis* Gold Mining Company, the Baron's name is Geldreich. The color of gold bathes the whole story in its rich light and there are many discreet parallels between fish and metal—a fish taken from the bank always finds its way back, and, as Henry and the Baron both know, fish once dead must be pickled, never interred. Christina Stead works out a neat idea with finesse, and the light, bantering tone creates a deliciously poised irony. It is hard to imagine a story of this kind better written.

For contrast we may take another short tale in a different vein, "Day of Wrath." This story, only three pages in length and told in the first person, concerns a woman divorced for adultery (her husband was a Cabinet Minister, rich, coarse and tyrannical) and living with her two children and her lover in a waterside village. The husband abandons all three to poverty.

The ladies were indignant that she continued to live in our district. "She should have at least the delicacy to go where she is not known," said my maiden aunt. Society, great beast of tender skin, blind, with elephant ears, felt indignant, lashed its little tail, and got hot around the rump. It required a sacrifice, and when Jumbo wants something the gods themselves obey. (p. 465)

Viola her fourteen year old daughter is one of the thirty children (all from the village) drowned when the local ferry is sunk in a collision with an ocean liner. "It seemed to my mother and aunt," says the boy-narrator, "that this was the 'judgment of God'; though for what mortal sins the other bereaved women had been punished, no one thought to conjecture" (p. 466). The story ends with the discovery of the girl's body; the simple eloquence of the final incident endorses the poetic justice of the outcome.

At the end of a week Viola was found on one end of the wreck, standing upright, uninjured, her right foot simply entangled in a rope. The founts of pity at this word broke their seals and jetted in each breast, and everyone that night had before his eye the image of Viola standing in the green gloom for a week, upright, looking for the rescuers, astonished that they did not come for her, perhaps with a lively word on her lips at their slowness, and then, prisoned by her poor weak foot, decaying, but with her arms still floating up; a watermaiden tangled in a lily-root, and not able to reach the surface. I cried and thought how she died in that attitude to ask pity.

In fact, it turned out that way; or at least, if the church and justice were not moved, for they should be above the frailties of flesh and blood, the women began to lament on her mother's account, to say she was well punished and one could even pity her. The beast was appeased, as in ancient days, by the sacrifice of a virgin. (pp. 466–67)

The first of the longer pair is "The Triskelion," a kind of case history pieced together from various sources by the narrator, a doctress at the hospital where the blind youth Arnold has been a patient. As he leaves he gives her a round gold medal he once found which has as its device three legs radiating from a small circle. Arnold marries a young immigrant girl who after eighteen months turns him out of the house because he is not "natural." A woman barrister, noticing the medal, tells of her frightening childhood experiences of the triskelion, a curious wheel-shaped phantom whose appearance at a coastal resort always foreshadows crime or terrible accident. Gradually the horrifying story of the rich but degraded Jenkins family emerges—a tale of murder and incest, of which the degenerate Arthur is the fruit. From another source comes a sequel of further evil and jealousy between mother and daughter. Such a summary account as this fails to do justice to the story. It has to be read and reread for the strangely compelling sense of horror and evil it generates; the supernatural touches help by creating an area of mystery in which normal human sanctions need not apply.

The second of this pair is "In Doulcemer." The narrator Arthur Field goes to see a tight-rope dancer perform on a wire stretched between two mountains above a decayed old village. On the way he meets an old acquaintance Charles Hodd, who writes about the village of Doulcemer and the artists' colony there for the New York *Gazette*. Hodd and his wife Sophie have gone back to nature and with other artists are now teaching the peasants the original arts of dyeing and weaving, which fell into disuse during the war. Another outsider is Nina Nyiregyhaza, who sells real estate (damp old cottages) to the artists and who has set up an agency for cloth and primitive pottery in Paris. Nina is a nasty, interfering busybody, always on the make, pretentious and fey. Sophie continually tells stories, all unpleasant, about Nina—how she encourages cats and how Stepan (her husband) is sent to throw the kittens she cannot give away over the cliff; how she exploits everybody, fawns before the local aristocracy, and scours the

countryside in search of purges for Stepan's constipation. As
Sophie truly says, Doulcemer is a place for malicious gossip. So
she prattles on while Charles laments that they are lost and that
only the Ninas survive here. Then, as they watch the tight-rope
performer:

"Each one of us is like that," said Charles, "balancing on as thin
a cord between precipice and precipice."
"It seems to me more like Doulcemer," said Sophie, "suspended in
the air precariously between its peaks. Scatter-brained colony doing
a polka in thin air."

And the story ends, baldly, banally:

At this moment the tight-rope performer put an end to all this bad
poetry by plunging headfirst into the chasm and coming to rest, calm
as could be, on the rocks at the bottom. (p. 155)

This story has the savage irony that characterizes certain of
Christina Stead's maturer work, *House of All Nations, The Man
Who Loved Children,* and (in its portrait of Jonathan Crow) *For
Love Alone.* The irony of "In Doulcemer" cuts both ways of
course, against the Ninas, exploiters and snobbish collectors of all
would-be geniuses, and against the Hodds, the pretentious (if
well-meaning) aesthetes, the self-deluding exiles doomed to frustration and failure. Indeed, Sophie becomes through her talk as
revolting as the woman she compulsively reviles.

"They say Nina's cat-hammed and potbellied, and that she wears
black stockings and rose-coloured garters nevertheless. She is ridicu-
lously affectionate to animals. She talks all day to five canaries, a
castrated cat and a frilled lizard she has in the house. Stepan loathes
animals. And as for Stepan, she looks after him like a baby: puts
aromatic oils over him to keep him in good health, bathes him and
powders him. He smells so sweet that the dogs and cows follow him
in the fields!" (p. 153)

XII   *The Element of Fantasy*

Barnard Eldershaw finds richness and strangeness the dominant
features of Christina Stead's first three books and argues for *The
Salzburg Tales* as the most successful of them because the writer's

inability to create living people matters less here than it does in a full-length novel. "No one develops beyond their initial statements. They are brilliant designs pinned up on the wall." [16] This is connected in Barnard Eldershaw's argument with Christina Stead's use of fantasy, which becomes almost the center of the critical analysis. Barnard Eldershaw's is a perceptive essay; much of the criticism she makes is fair, though she becomes so preoccupied with the fantasy that she overlooks or underestimates other things. We cannot justifiably expect more than sketches or suggestions for character in stories the length of most of these in *The Salzburg Tales*. And it can be maintained, furthermore, that we do get insight into people in *Seven Poor Men of Sydney*, even if the characters there are not solid and foursquare in the manner of the conventional novel. (No one should question the existence of "living characters" in the later novels.) Barnard Eldershaw's essay gives the impression that these early books offer little apart from the luxuriant growths of an over-fertile imagination, though she is fair enough to add in her discussion of the subject matter of *The Salzburg Tales* that "it is not fantasy in a world of fantasy, but fantasy in a world of reality and reality in a world of fantasy." [17]

The underlying reality of *Seven Poor Men of Sydney* and even *The Salzburg Tales* needs to be stressed. Clifton Fadiman describes *The Salzburg Tales* as consisting of "forty adult fairy stories"—"adult" is a key word here.[18] The four stories discussed above all make humanly significant statements. Even a story like "The Mirror," which owes much of its attractiveness to its frankly Gothic qualities, deals with matters as "real" in human experience as the sense of personality dissolving and the notion that we people the vacancies of the mirror world with images of ourselves.[19] Here the fantastic is linked with reality as in legends and fairy tales. Rarely, if ever, is it allowed to get out of hand in *The Salzburg Tales*. Its potential is suggested in a passage in *Seven Poor Men of Sydney* where Catherine, talking to Baruch, is analyzing Joseph.

"Joseph has no understanding whatever of the muscles and nerves of the world. So he rarely smiles, for he sees no humour, that is to say, no shifting of the natural order, no obscurity, gleam and veiling of the plain world in fancy." (p. 153)

Seen in this light fantasy is a means of insight and makes possible that humor which is the perception of incongruities. No one mature enough to understand fairy tales has ever believed that they provide only an escape from reality. *The Salzburg Tales* provides us with an apt quotation: "I only tell fairy-tales (said the Philosopher) for I would rather be seen in their sober vestments than in the prismatic unlikelihood of reality. Besides, every fairy-tale has a modern instance" (p. 231).

Christina Stead's detachment in *Seven Poor Men of Sydney* has, I believe, been underrated. It is an intensely felt book but there is no reason to suppose that the author identifies herself with the intensest, or for that matter, with any of the other characters. In fact, the book's structure and the positioning of its characters (and here Mendelssohn is useful) establish a sufficiently clear distance between the writer and her creations.[20] The detachment is even clearer in *The Salzburg Tales* (though the author's individual voice may still be heard) because the kind of book she has now chosen to write makes possible the artistic exploitation of different modes. Melodrama, for example, occurs, as in "Gaspard," an elaborate tale of love in conflict with social class in late eighteenth century France, in "The Gold Bride," and in "To the Mountain," not as some gratuitous emotional product but as a distinctive (and controlled) formal feature determining the romantic and legendary qualities of the tales. This kind of artistic make-believe is reinforced occasionally by the remarks of the listeners when the narration ends: the Gothic horrors of "To the Mountain" cause aggrieved and skeptical comments; so again the listeners protest against the Lawyer's story, the women on sentimental and the men on logical grounds. Bringing various points of view to bear in this way encourages a critical detachment in the reader also. Satire and parody we have already noted. It seems no coincidence that the Centenarist's tales which round off the narratives on the final day should include the wildest sort of spoofing about a family skeleton, which even the inventive Centenarist is hard put to justify.

The weaknesses of the book stem from high-spirited ingenuity rather than uncontrolled fantasy. Christina Stead falls at times into overelaboration. It is rash to dogmatize when, as here, it is a matter of degree, but "Speculation in Lost Causes," it might be said, carries on the complication of the details too long, even granting the fact that the smothering of justice and truth (by the versions of different witnesses) is the theme of the story. A similar fault may be urged against "Don Juan in the Arena" where in addition to over-ingenious extensions of the legend Christina Stead finds the colorful, exotic elements something of a temptation; the effect of this is, again, to stretch out the story too far.

The Salzburg Tales nevertheless remains a brilliant and highly original work. Not the least of its attractions is the variety of tone and mood it offers. Critics impressed by its more striking features have, however, often failed to observe that a substantial number of the stories (in fact, about a quarter) are in essence character studies realistically presented—for instance "The Little Old Lady," a subtle and allusive wisp of a tale, is rich in psychological implications; "Overcote" has all the ingredients of domestic tragedy and anticipates *The Man Who Loved Children,* which stands firmly in the great tradition of psychological Realism in European fiction. *The Salzburg Tales,* Barnard Eldershaw observes, sounds all notes from the ridiculous to the macabre—all, perhaps, but the sentimental, which never appears in Christina Stead's work, except as a subject for satire. The range of subject and mood and their firmer control make *The Salzburg Tales* artistically superior to (if less moving than) *Seven Poor Men of Sydney.* In both books reality and fantasy jostle and mingle; in the novel this shifting of focus and superimposing of planes is an accompaniment to tragedy; in the short stories the effects are more varied, ironic or light-hearted more often than tragic. In Christina Stead's next book *The Beauties and Furies* the relationship between reality and fantasy becomes more precarious.

CHAPTER 3

Paris: Love and Money

O NLY two years separate the publication of *The Beauties and Furies* from that of *House of All Nations*, but so great is the difference between these two novels of life in Paris that we are justified in taking the latter as a turning point in Christina Stead's literary career. *The Beauties and Furies* is her poorest book, but significant in a number of ways. It shows a young writer struggling to expand; not content to fall back on her previous successes, she is on the lookout for fresh subjects. In some respects it harks back to *Seven Poor Men of Sydney* and *The Salzburg Tales;* in others it further anticipates themes, already foreshadowed in the first book, which will receive fuller and better treatment in *House of All Nations, For Love Alone,* and as far ahead as *Letty Fox.* Standing between the early and the later works *The Beauties and Furies* is a strange mixture which, though it has its moments, never succeeds in fusing its elements into one consistent whole. For the present the memories of Australia, it seems, are written out and Christina Stead now turns from the tales told at Salzburg to write about Eruope again but this time in a full-length novel of student life and love in Paris.

In an interview in 1935 already referred to, Christina Stead after discussing *Seven Poor Men of Sydney* is quoted as saying: "My next work of fiction is to be *Student Lovers*—a book containing two or three short novels, of which one, at least, begins in Sydney. This one is *The Travelling Scholar*. These three short novels are, in a sense, love stories." [1] This original plan did not work out—*The Beauties and Furies is* a book about a student lover, the naïve and self-centered young socialist Oliver Fenton and his mistress Elvira Western, but it has grown beyond the scope of a nouvelle. The other projected short novel, *The Travelling Scholar,* obviously grew into the longer (and different) story *For Love Alone,* which was not published till 1944.

I The Beauties and Furies: *The Story*

The story of *The Beauties and Furies* (whatever may be said of the style in certain places) is ordinary enough. Oliver, handsome, vain and irresponsible, believes he is freeing Elvira from the chains of a bourgeois marriage. Elvira abandons her devoted but dull husband Dr. Paul Western in England, and joins Oliver, who is on a scholarship in Paris. Elvira, though an honors graduate in Arts, has no interest in the politics which Oliver is studying or in the socialism which he (supposedly) is practicing. Despite the excitement of having burnt all her boats and elected for romance, she is not attracted to Paris itself either, and as the story develops she comes to realize the hollowness of her relationship with Oliver. One simple reason for its failure (the main one is Oliver's selfishness) is that she is five years older than he and has eight years of married life with Paul behind her.

In the very first chapter there enters into their lives the strange lace-buyer Annibale Marpurgo, fantast and dandy. The middle-aged Marpurgo, who has an invalid wife he rarely sees, interests himself in the affairs of the young couple and makes the appealing suggestion that Oliver should go into the lace business and make money. Elvira's troubles really begin when she becomes pregnant; after much self-torment she finally decides to accept the advice of Blanche, a French actress Oliver has introduced her to, and have an abortion. Elvira's doubts are increased by the arrival in Paris of a trio of would-be-helpers—the ever sympathetic Paul, his cousin Sara, and Elvira's brother Adam. Marpurgo wants Paul to take Elvira back to England and now does all he can to discredit Oliver in the eyes of the world. The main reason for this is jealousy; Marpurgo has grown fond of the beautiful Coromandel, a young lace-designer with whom Oliver (an incorrigible philanderer) is conducting an affair. But, Elvira having settled for Oliver, abortion, and poverty, Paul returns home defeated. Marpurgo and Oliver both woo Coromandel and the scheming Marpurgo arranges for Coromandel to discover Oliver's attachment to Elvira. As matters worsen for him Oliver turns to Blanche for amorous consolation. Elvira finally learns about Oliver's hypocritical betrayal of her and, completely disillusioned, returns to London. Oliver now takes up with Blanche but she leaves him once his money runs out. Marpurgo (by means of money extracted from

Paul) arranges for Oliver to go back to England. The final, ironic
scene shows Oliver, who has been drifting helplessly for months,
as his old self again, cutting an impressive figure for a beautiful
young girl composer he meets on the train. As the book ends he is
offering her some of his poems to be set to music.

II *Types of Character*

Looking back over these first three books we can now see certain key characters and ideas emerging and the continuous shaping
of a few basic themes. One of the dominant character types, who
is to undergo further development later on but who, in his early
form, is taken about as far as possible in *The Beauties and Furies*,
is the Munchausen-figure, the liar and fantasist, the erudite and
obscene spellbinder.[2] At his most realistic he appears as Withers
in *Seven Poor Men of Sydney*, where, despite his strange qualities,
he is set firmly in the prosaic environment of Chamberlain's printing works; on a restricted scale (because here there is no suggestion of evil) he comes into *The Salzburg Tales* as the Centenarist,
the man of recondite learning and innumerable stories; and finally
he appears in *The Beauties and Furies* as the grotesque and sometimes repulsive Marpurgo, who like Withers is a schemer but a
less comprehensible one.

The second important type is the tyrannical father. Once again
Seven Poor Men of Sydney is the original source—this time not in
the shape of a character but in a general description by Kol
Blount.

"Your ideal man is not the balanced, fire-hearted liberal, dripping
with humanity and sweetness, who loves his enemies because they
are men, weeps and fights for pacifism, employs the poor, encourages
talent, educates children, and rules his family life like a patriarch;
who never vails his crest, blunts his word; who crushes egotism, but
pursues his own will through thick and thin; who believes in morality,
but runs with a bunch of nettles to clear the haunts of superstition;
who reveals hypocrisy even if it rises in his dearest friend?" (p. 60)

This type occurs in "Overcote" (*The Salzburg Tales*) as the self-
advertising free-thinker, the boastful, egoistic schoolmaster who
denies his children independence, spoils their chances of marriage
and a career, and in his old age gives way to self-pity because they
have turned from him; in *For Love Alone* as Andrew, head of the

Hawkins family, from whose bonds Teresa must free herself; and in *The Man Who Loved Children* as Sam Pollit, the soupy, domineering, egocentric idealist to whom *The Beauties and Furies* carries no clear analogue.

The third important type to emerge is that of the young woman, trying to break free of the bonds of custom and tradition in order to achieve self-realization. First in this group is Catherine in *Seven Poor Men of Sydney* who is to all appearances emancipated, since she has cast off family ties and all the claims of respectability and given herself (but spasmodically) to the socialist cause. Yet Catherine, unlike Teresa, never achieves fulfilment as a woman—she understands herself well enough but cannot resolve her problems; as she says at the end, she is a woman trying to be a man. In this respect she differs from Elvira, though they have in common a discontent and a desire for a richer life. Elvira is half a rebel—enough to take the first steps to freedom, only to find that she is basically unadventurous and ideologically a thorough bourgeois. In a moment of insight she tries to make Oliver see the truth, but he cannot or will not admit it. " 'That's what we are, you see: suburban, however wild we run. You know quite well, in yourself, don't you, two people like us can't go wild? Still it's nice to pretend to, for a while.' " [3] Allowing for certain individual differences, Baruch's drawing "La Femme s'échappe de la Forêt" in *Seven Poor Men of Sydney* symbolizes Elvira's as well as Catherine's plight; as he spells it out to Joseph: " 'Woman escapes from the forest. It means, the middle-class woman trying to free herself, and still impeded by romantic notions and ferocious, because ambushed, sensuality' " (p. 155).

III   *Theme. Relationship to Other Novels*

This passage points to the center of *The Beauties and Furies*, toward a theme which is in danger of being obscured by the antics and the rhetorical extravagances of Marpurgo. The most interesting aspect of this theme is the idea of freedom in and through love and the difficulty of realizing it in modern society. " 'The real thought of the middle-class woman,' complained Elvira, 'is the problem of economic freedom and sexual freedom: they can't be attained at the same time' " (p. 127). And Elvira, more honest in self-analysis than Oliver ever could be, terrifies him by admitting as a reason for coming to him: ". . . I just

wanted to see, if in continuing in my own line, you know, just
peering, being curious, analysing, being objective, even in love,
and I am, I could get any new experiences'" (p. 77). Again in a
passage that clearly anticipates the dilemma that Teresa, a more
courageous woman, faces and at least partially resolves, she says,
"'I find there is no such thing as a spiritual renaissance, at least
not for a woman. We are too much nailed to a coffin of flesh, our
souls are only plants, they are rooted in an earth of flesh. We need
a home, security, comfort for our flesh before the mind can
grow'" (p. 170). And (once more reminding us of Teresa) she
can still say, wistfully, at the end of her bitter experience: "'I
suppose a woman, to be completely rounded, should taste a lot of
men's individualities: in a way I believe in free love'" (p. 339).

There are numerous other points of resemblance to *Seven Poor
Men of Sydney* and anticipations of *For Love Alone*—indeed *The
Beauties and Furies* may well have been useful in an uninten-
tional way as a sorting ground for some of the later work. The
counterpart of Catherine, "a woman of revolution without a barricade," is Oliver, "an arm-chair revolutionary." Oliver is, too, a
sham socialist not unlike the Folliots, though they of course have
more money. More importantly, Oliver is clearly an early version
of Jonathan Crow, Teresa's idealized man in *For Love Alone*, who
plays with her affection and loyalty in his cold, selfish way. Crow,
like Oliver, fancies himself as an intellectual, but both are second-
rate eclectics, shallow poseurs, who toy with people as with the
ideas they manage to pick up from their reading. Another
(minor) parallel occurs between Adam, Elvira's brother, and
Quick, the American, who helps to rescue Teresa from Crow; both
these men like to woo in erotic images drawn from Carew's poetry
—indeed, Adam once had a mistress named Teresa. The search
for love and freedom is far more moving in *For Love Alone*,
partly because Teresa is a more interesting and attractive character than Elvira. This personal theme, nonetheless, accounts for
the best parts of *The Beauties and Furies.*

IV   *Some Critical Opinions*

The *Sydney Morning Herald* reviewer received *The Beauties
and Furies* fairly favorably.[4] The "artificial style" which marked
Seven Poor Men of Sydney and "a leaning towards redundancy"
mar "a definite flair for delineation of character and a good sense

of dialogue and situation." He says, rightly, that Elvira is well-drawn, an exasperating person but justly handled. He believes (taking refuge in vagueness here) that Oliver, Adam, Coromandel, and Marpurgo all run true to form and that the balance between them is well-preserved. Finally, he says that the book is too long, that the last third flags and that the author needs a firmer grasp of the principles of construction. Parts of this are surprising—notably the failure to observe any essential differences between Marpurgo and Coromandel on the one hand and the other leading characters, and the implication that *The Beauties and Furies* is as good a book as *Seven Poor Men of Sydney*.

Even more favorable are the comments by Roderick, in a brief survey of Christina Stead's work up to 1946, which begin: "The story is told to an obbligato of stinging satire and sharp irony. Its humour is marked by asperity and cynicism. Its dialogue, while at times marred by cloying richness of imagery or by metaphysical concettism resulting in needless obscurity, amply reveals the cultural background of the characters. Exuberance of expression in both dialogue and narrative runs parallel with a striking power of conveying emotional and psychic states in vivid prose." [5]

At the other extreme to Roderick's is the view put forward by Barnard Eldershaw, in an essay which deals with only the first three of Christina Stead's books, that *The Beauties and Furies* is the one clear failure. Barnard Eldershaw is, I believe, closer to the truth though, characteristically, she overstates the case against the book. As indicated above, her argument is that Christina Stead's real talent lies in fantasy and therefore she cannot create living characters; *The Salzburg Tales* is the most successful because her limitations do not matter in his kind of work; *Seven Poor Men of Sydney* suffers from the application of "a fantastic, half-grotesque technique to a rational theme" but is saved from the full consequence of this because its weight is thrown on the social rather than the individual element in it. "But," Barnard Eldershaw continues, "in *The Beauties and Furies*, which is an intimate and individual study of a small group of people, the very life of the book depends upon its characterization. No amount of meretricious glitter can animate these sawdust puppets, so that for all its undiminished surface brilliance the book fails, and fails helplessly." [6]

V   *The Problem of the Grotesques*

The Beauties and Furies is by no means such an utter failure. For one thing Elvira is not a puppet; nor for that matter (though less well presented) is Oliver; even Blanche, a rather stagey creature, has her moments of individuality (as, indeed, Barnard Eldershaw later admits). The real trouble lies, rather, with characters like Marpurgo and (to a lesser extent) Coromandel, who do not function on the same level as the realistically presented characters. Elvira, Oliver, and Paul live fairly commonplace lives and the reader accepts them as they come—in realistic terms; what jolts him is the way Marpurgo, who seems to have come from an altogether different world, is brought into this area of ordinary human relationships and made to operate there. Marpurgo is such a grotesque that any attempts to explain his initial interference in the lives of ordinary people like Elvira and Oliver (even if we are prepared to accept jealousy of Oliver as a motive later on) are bound to fail. Perplexed by his continual obtrusiveness Elvira on one occasion asks him why he torments them, and gets this for an answer:

"I'm a virtuoso in decadence, disintegration, mental necrosis: if I sit at home, I corrode myself: I can't work in a vacuum. Out, I gather little eschatalogical flowers to meditate in the hectic nights of the bacillus of Koch. Each of your sorrows is for me an hour of nepenthe: in that hour I build up an endoped dome of misery and failure, doubt and dissolution, ridicule and insufficiency beyond inferno, Eblis, opium, Xanadu. . . ." (pp. 295–96)

Marpurgo is a grotesque in the Romantic, fin-de-siècle, not the Dickensian, manner and once launched into speech he is apt to rave. Christina Stead refers in one place to "the learned farrago" he goes on with, but the reader can never be sure whether to take him seriously or not; certainly, he is not presented in a consistently satirical way. In his relationship to Elvira and Oliver he emerges as a rather repulsive grub who feeds on the intimacies of other people's lives, leaving his slime upon them but never satisfying his appetite. Furthermore, and this is what makes him all the more difficult to accept, he is used as observer and commentator, a role for which his personality makes him unsuitable; the reader needs a more normal, reliable person as a guide.

Toward the end of the book Marpurgo bitterly denounces Oliver to his face as a weak, egoistic, cowardly, vain man, "an inkpot-valiant," and then goes on to describe himself as a somnambulist on the brink of insanity. This chapter is to end with the wildly fantastic scene at the Somnambulist Club, but not before Marpurgo has been required to pass judgment (on the novelist's behalf) upon Oliver.

"You are a dead soul Oliver. You are fooling yourself with all these ideas of revolutions and these friendships with revolutionaries. It doesn't fool anyone but you. . . . You are corrupt like me. You can't be the workers' friend: you'd deceive them as you deceived your other friend—Dr. Western. You've got to be like me. You've got to be a mealymouth." (p. 323)

And as the book ends Marpurgo again sums up, this time on the relationship between Elvira and Oliver: " 'She was just a spell of blessed self-forgetfulness for an academic drudge' " (p. 365).

If we detach Marpurgo from the surroundings of an everyday story and examine him as a kind of gargoyle, he represents quite an achievement of the imagination. He seems to have stepped straight from one of the frankly fantastic sequences in *The Salzburg Tales*, where he could have been in harmony with his surroundings, into a book which must depend finally on its analysis of a more or less commonplace personal relationship between a phoney scholar and a frustrated housewife. Marpurgo tells Paul in his characteristically high falutin way that he was attracted to Elvira because he saw in her an unusual woman in an unusual situation; but all the other evidence suggests that she is a rather ordinary woman caught in an awkward situation. She is certainly not the rare beauty Marpurgo or Oliver would have us believe; for this kind of exotic we have to turn to Coromandel.

A bizarre atmosphere surrounds the early Coromandel sequences and the attempt to link them with the Elvira–Oliver story creates a sense of incongruity. In themselves the scenes at Paindebled's have a grotesque brilliance which is startling, even fascinating, but they are acceptable only as isolated set-pieces. There is a similarly haunting, fantastic quality in the white grotesqueries of the Arnhem chapters in *Letty Fox* but there the poetic force of the scenes is functionally justified because it creates the disturbing

VI Paris: The Financial World

Moving from *The Beauties and Furies* to *House of All Nations*, from love without money to love of money, is like going from Baudelaire to Balzac and for a novelist this is a step in the right direction. It is Paris again but no longer the enchanting city, home of artists and intellectuals, of lovers and prostitutes who (to Oliver's delight) quote Baudelaire while on the beat; it is the Paris of big business and finance, the city of the capitalist barons and the stock exchange speculators. It is Baudelaire's "Fourmillante cité, cité pleine de rêves"—with a difference, for now the dreams are those of the money-makers. Yet *House of All Nations* depicts a life in its own way almost as fantastic as that of Marpurgo's wildest imaginings despite its thoroughly realistic documentation of modern society. It is a kind of twentieth-century *Arabian Nights*, and the genie it conjures up is money.[8] The description of the Banker in *The Salzburg Tales* is an early sketch of Jules Bertillon in *House of All Nations*. To all appearances a man of the world, Jules lives out his fantasies in his own charming, irresponsible way, responding to calls on his humanity only when he feels in the mood—a prince in a modern fairy tale, who wants to surround himself with gold because it is such a lovely color. The final irony of this epic of money and money-making is that when Jules at last absconds, after having made and lost his millions several times over, the magistrates are unable to discover anything definite about the Banque Mercure, its assets and its operations. It is not as if a great solid structure has collapsed, but rather that the structure is now shown to be what it always was—a shell floating on air. Living in exile (and luxury) with his whole family in Estonia Jules is asked by reporters if he can account for the bank's closing, and his reply is: " 'Oh, I should just say it closed from absence of liquidity: a not uncommon weakness with banks nowadays.' " And what happened to the rest of the money? " 'You know how those things are! The money just went!' " (p. 772). Mercurial is certainly the word for Jules and his organization.

House of All Nations is a long, densely packed novel of 787 pages, which through its account of the day-to-day life at the bank, Bertillon Frères, seeks to describe the whole business of money-making and its attendant robbery and jobbery in the Paris of the early 1930's. Many books have been written about the search for wealth and power, about misers and millionaires, but few can compare with *House of All Nations* for its authentic and detailed knowledge of what actually goes on behind the scenes, where plans are laid, hunches seized upon, and transactions pushed through. Jules's way of running a bank is, to say the least, unconventional—in fact, he has operated illegally for years on a contre-partie basis, which means, simply, playing the market with his clients' stock in the hope of making big profits. Some of his wealthy clients know or suspect this but are prepared to trust his cool nerve and his genius for gambling. His personality and reputation attract all sorts of people (with all sorts of financial projects) to the bank to do business or just to talk money. Jules is the most important character, but *House of All Nations* is not a novel built round a central figure and treating a certain occupation or social group. Money is a great leveller and in *House of All Nations* there is room for all sorts and classes of men: merchants, economists, lawyers, accountants, bankers, clerks, managers, clients, tellers, customers' men, typists, magistrates, cashiers, industrial magnates, deputies, jurists, brokers and rentiers—and a more miscellaneous bunch of secret go-betweens, shysters, imaginary employees, swindlers, stalking-horses, prostitutes, playboys, servants, family cadgers, society figures, writers, artists, Communists, cronies, philanderers, and mistresses galore. It is Balzacian in its precise observation, in its accumulation of detail, and in its insistence upon the driving force of human obsession. A novel conceived on such a scale will obviously pose formal problems.

VII House of All Nations: *Structure and Plot*

The following passage from a review Christina Stead once wrote of Louis Aragon's *The Century Was Young* touches on the characteristics and, by implication, the difficulties of the long novel in our day. The analysis of *House of All Nations* that follows it will show how she has tried to avoid the dangers, as she sees them, of this kind of book.

Very interesting are two characteristics of long modern novels, exhibited also in this one. All modern artists seem strangely to feel that they are near Judgment Day. They are making summaries of their times and some sink their craft under a load of detail, like the great Joyce and the little Romains; and many, many give us novels of Begat, where we are obliged to run the course from great-grandfather to great-grandson, with the idea of explaining why we are where we are to-day; as though it were necessary to start with Pliny's maps to sail to Japan today. As a result, the hero-with-the-notebook has also come to the fore, dignified brother of the star-reporter-gangbuster.[9]

How is the novelist to organize great masses of material? Thackeray solves the problem in his panoramic *Vanity Fair* by placing two heroines in society and playing off one's fluctuating fortunes against the other's, so that when Becky is on the crest of a wave, Amelia is down in a trough and vice versa. As in *Seven Poor Men of Sydney* Christina Stead has tried in *House of All Nations* to devise the kind of form the book needs. Instead of chopping the material into longish chapter blocks of about the same length she casts it into a number of separate scenes (104 in all) which vary in length according to their importance between two and forty-two pages. Since there is no attempt to construct a series of complicated interlocking stories in the Dickens manner in order to bring numerous characters into relationship with one another, the material can come through in the form of scenes without the jerkiness that would become apparent in a more closely plotted novel. The only connection the minor characters need to have is the cash nexus which links them to the Banque Mercure. This, of course, would not suffice for the main characters; a small group, roughly equal in importance, is to the fore throughout—the Bertillon brothers, Jules and William, the bank economist Michel Alphendéry, the wealthy Dr. Jacques Carrière, the grain merchant Henri Léon, the customers' man Aristide Raccamond and his ruthless, scheming wife Marianne. It is with these that the narrative is concerned and the story itself is simple enough.

The first scene introduces Raccamond, middle-aged, ambitious, and well meaning, in his old-maidish manner. Raccamond was once customers' man at Claude Brothers private bank, recently liquidated, and is now trying to worm his way into Bertillon Frères. Despite Jules's initial distrust of him Raccamond gets the position he wants, partly because he succeeds in persuading Henri Léon to become one of Jules's clients. Jules's instincts about Raccamond were right, as the concluding stages of the novel prove.

In the meanwhile the wealthy Carrière, whose favors Raccamond has been cultivating for some time, comes upon the scene.

Carrière is Jules's most bitter enemy. He is a dissolute homosexual, whose jealousy of Jules stems from their schooldays together. Carrière is bent on destroying Jules. In the course of a business talk Jules rashly bets Carrière that the pound sterling will not fall below 122 francs. An agreement is signed whereby if it does Jules will pay Carrière at that rate on all drafts submitted. It so happens that a careless phrase in the document gives Carrière the whip hand, for when sterling does fall (as Jules's most reliable friends predicted to him that it would) Jules finds himself obliged to pay out large regular sums in connection with a brewery in England that has come into Carrière's possession. And these payments will have to continue unless Jules can disprove Carrière's assertion that the brewery has been sold.[10] Carrière bleeds Jules mercilessly, the European slump sets in and Jules, faced with a copy of the agreement with Carrière and letters concerning payments which William at last gets hold of, is forced to admit the truth he has been denying to his brother and Alphendéry for months past.

Matters are now brought to a head by Carrière's toady Raccamond who, genuinely worried about the security of his customers' investments, discovers private ledgers at the bank's Brussels office which reveal the extent of Jules's contrepartie operations over the years. Having bribed his way into possession of these ledgers Raccamond goes almost berserk in rage and self-righteous indignation and tries to blackmail Jules into restoring the share positions of his clients and giving him a partnership with special privileges, which would make him virtual controller of the bank. Raccamond, spurred on by Carrière and Marianne, manages by the violence of his behavior to antagonize almost everybody involved, though (ironically) his cause is basically just. For the first time in his life Jules is thoroughly rattled; he makes half-hearted plans to strike back but he is losing his grip. He has by now turned from his best friends, William and Alphendéry, and has sunk large sums in a crazy aviation combine started by a group of young aristocrats who fail to bring in the money they are supposed to provide, and finally takes the step he has been talking about for months by closing the bank and clearing out with all the money he can lay his hands on.

The consequent public enquiry gets nowhere; people refuse to talk, records are destroyed, broils develop between clients; most people prefer a Jules to a Raccamond anyhow. All the remaining assets are disappearing and, by the end, the Banque Mercure S. A. creditors are paying 208 lawyers. Alphendéry, now working for Léon, receives a telegram from William to say Jules has disappeared, and asking Alphendéry to try to trace him. But no one knows where Jules has gone, and the book ends:

His old friends, and even the most pertinacious of the creditors, hoped that he went and made immediately a shining new fortune with which he would come home presently to flash in their eyes. For he had by now benefited by the immorality as well as by the mythomania of the financial world and had begun to be relacquered in the minds of the rich. For others, though, it is true, he still remained a rankle and a hurt, the charmer who deceived. (p. 787)

House of All Nations is Christina Stead's greatest intellectual achievement—its knowledge of the workings of international finance and its revelation of the fraud, the ruthlessness, the energy, the sheer luck, and the genius that go into money-making, are by any standards remarkable. So detailed is this knowledge in the account of Léon's great scheme for making a fortune out of wheat deals that the reader almost needs to be a professional economist himself to follow the incredibly complex maneuvers, even with the aid of Alphendéry's patient explanations to Jules. This is to say that *House of All Nations* will never be as widely read and enjoyed as some of the other books. But for all its intellectual qualities it is a deeply felt novel too. It is less idiosyncratic in style and tone than its predecessors. One instance of the change is the overwhelming preponderance of dialogue—dialogue, furthermore, of the naturalistic rather than expressionistic kind, in keeping with the method of scenic presentation. Here Christina Stead shows she can write dialogue that establishes character by differentiation. Léon is a superbly realized figure, so too are Raccamond and Jules. If Alphendéry does not measure up to them it is, possibly, because of the double role of actor-raisonneur allotted to him. On the question of dialogue one of the early reviewers, Edwin Berry Burgum makes the point that the volume of talk is in itself a protective device. "When every contradictory impulse is laid bare, no onlooker can tell for certain which will get translated into action." But, Burgum says, speech and action become one and he goes on to quote a remark made by the Comtesse de Voigrand to Jules: " 'There are poor men in this country who cannot be bought; the day I found that out, I sent my gold abroad.' " And he comments: "This avowal of her social idealism is not an abstract witticism from Rochefoucauld, but the recollection of an order to her banker." [11]

VIII   *Links with the Early Books*

House of All Nations is precisely the sort of book that Barnard Eldershaw, judging by her essay, would believe Christina Stead incapable of writing. Today the critic, with the wisdom of hindsight if all else is lacking, ought to be able to observe that its difference from the two previous novels, striking though it may be, is one more of manner and degree than of basic themes and attitudes. A critical view of individuals and of society at large is present in both *Seven Poor Men of Sydney* and *The Beauties and Furies,* and irony colors many of the stories in *The Salzburg Tales.* These elements combine to create the dominant tone of *House of All Nations.* The most characteristic feature of Christina Stead's fiction as a whole is not the fantasy stressed by her early critics but its emotional intensity, the concentrated gaze that sees through appearances and illusions. It is this uncompromising honesty which will help the best of her work to endure—it makes possible the unforgettable Jonathan Crow and Sam Pollit and it gives conviction to the sufferings of the women, Teresa and Henrietta, who are bound to them. This intensity is first fully experienced in *House of All Nations.* Where in modern fiction could we find anything to surpass the controlled ferocity of "A Stuffed Carp," one of the most memorable scenes in a book that is Jonsonian in its exposure of greed, graft, and exploitation?

In addition to an early sketch of Jules in the figure of the Banker, *The Salzburg Tales* also provides us with an embryonic Henri Léon in the person of Henry Van Laer in "The Amenities." Van Laer, like Léon, has a rapid, unnatural way of speaking and uses frequent, impetuous gestures. Again like Léon he has an insatiable appetite for women. The Léon character, the dynamic, untutored money-making genius seems to have fascinated our author; he turns up again, with certain modifications, in the protagonist of *A Little Tea, a Little Chat,* Robbie Grant. Furthermore, the main woman in Léon's floating harem, the shrewd, calculating blonde Mrs. Weyman, foreshadows the larger-scale portrait of

Barbara, Robbie's blondine. A final link occurs in Alphendéry—economist, leftist, a student (unlike Oliver) with compassion instead of ink in his veins, supremely articulate, who might almost be the Baruch Mendelssohn of *Seven Poor Men of Sydney* moved from the United States to Paris and given a European upbringing.

IX *The Title*

All nationalities come to the Banque Mercure and so it is in an obvious way a house of all nations; the critics who have discussed the book seem to assume that the title refers merely to the Bertillon bank. But the title phrase occurs only twice in the text and each time the allusion is to the high-class Parisian brothel also referred to in Nathanael West's *A Cool Million*. The phrase is first used in *Scene Two* where William says to Alphendéry that (despite Jules's opposition) they would be foolish to reject Raccamond because of his bad reputation of crawling to the rich and serving their vices. " 'We've got a man to buy tickets for the bouts for clients: I don't see why we can't have a man who knows the prices at the House of All Nations!' " (p. 29).

It occurs again about half-way through the book when Léon tells Alphendéry at the bank that he has lost a batch of important letters in the House of All Nations or, maybe, at his hotel (p. 388). The bank and the brothel are equated—in both, man's concupiscence is given free rein.

X *Jules*

Jules has no doubts as to what the motive force behind a bank is. " 'It's easy to make money. You put up the sign BANK and someone walks in and hands you his money. The façade is everything.' " This is a characteristic remark; Jules is a thorough skeptic (if not a cynic). Despite his affection for Alphendéry (which, be it noted, does not survive the collapse of the bank) Jules is unable to understand Alphendéry's attachment to humanitarian and political ideals. Jules, in the Balzac manner, is a character built around one dominating idea—the notion that informs his whole philosophy and way of life is that money is the measure of all things. Yet there are other facets to his personality; he is by nature charming and gay, generous and irresponsible, knowing that he can afford to throw his money about because he can always make another fortune.

Like Arthur Miller's Willie Loman he wants not only to be liked but also to be well-liked, and being self-centered is prone to find in his friends indifference and insults where none exist. He is quick-witted and shrewd, but without an ounce of intellect in his make-up—that is why he cannot understand Alphendéry. Like all gamblers he is superstitious and given to hunches and therefore apt to be taken in by flatterers, especially those like the foolish and incompetent Bomba who have the actor's panache.

Jules is an incorrigible liar and a self-deceiver—in time of crisis he is the despair of William and Alphendéry, who do all the hard work and try to save the bank from the consequences of his folly and whose only reward is ingratitude. Furthermore, like all true egoists he can be nasty and petty. In pique he ruins Léon's great wheat scheme, which has the promise of fortunes, because he has not thought of it himself or, more accurately, because he does not really understand it and could never have invented such a brilliant plan himself. Life for Jules is a masquerade but he revels in it and in his best moods his enjoyment is infectious. This is his strength—he dominates by his charm.

Jules is a successful creation because the attractive and the repellent qualities lie side by side with perfect congruity in the one character. Alphendéry's affection for him is thoroughly credible even though he is disturbed by Jules's lack of moral responsibility. Alphendéry sees in Jules a creative talent corrupted and more than once pleads with him to abandon his fantasies and come back to the earth. "Fantasies" is the right word, for Alphendéry with true insight senses that Jules does not really want all the money he is continually dreaming of; as the author says, ". . . he cared not so much for money as for moneymaking, and, when he had got the hang of moneymaking, not so much the making of money as the endless field for speculation and fantasy it yielded him" (p. 597).

A life given over to the pursuit of riches seems to Alphendéry like chasing phantoms, because riches as such have no social value; a true socialist, Alphendéry looks for wealth, which is productive. Jules likes to consider himself a magician; he believes (or says) that big money is won, never earned, but Alphendéry pricks this sort of bubble-blowing easily: "'What a race of liars you all are! . . . You work day and night at your schemes and then you love to pretend it's all pure luck; you just lie on your back with

your mouth open and luck throws in *pâté de foie gras'* " (p. 311).
The idea is significant, nonetheless, of the fantasy Jules indulges
in.

XI   *The Dialogue*

The verbal energy and inventiveness, which takes some strange
forms in the previous books, is now being poured into highly articulate dialogue and it is the dialogue which gives vitality and
interest to the principal characters. Rich and copious, their speech
never lets them down. Since Jules has been under discussion, passages relating to him will serve doubly as illustrations. Here is
Jules, in the scene already quoted from:

"I'm not an old maid playing patience. I want big money and what
have I got round me? Savers, hoarders, go-gentlies, abacus gentry
back in the carpetbags of the Middle Ages, squirrels, ants, census
takers, pennybank campaigners—installment-plan robbers, shilling-a-
week shortchangers, Saturday tillshakers, busfare embezzlers, dime
defalcators—you're as bad as Etienne. You're honest. It's no good hid-
ing it. All your philosophy hasn't got you farther than scraping and
pinching, like the knifegrinder's wife. If you start little, you remain
little. If you start with bells on, you end with bells on. I know what
I want. I only want to hear from you how it's to be done. You're my
technical expert, Michel. I employ you for that. Go to Maître Lemaître
or Beaubien and find out how to do it. That's all I'm asking you."
(p. 201)

Here is Jules again, talking to Raccamond, who is worried about
the bank's reputation:

"Raccamond, every woman is a whore, but the whores are the ones
who never learned the game: every banker is a poker shark but the
Eddie McCaheys are the poor fellows who don't get away with it.
What is a whore? A poor girl who never had a chance to go into
business with a man and set up a little home of her own. The same
with the little swindlers. I'm sorry for them. Haven't you got a heart,
Raccamond? Are you all for profit, dignity, reputation? Have you
forgotten what sort of business you're in? You'll turn into a crank
if you're not careful. And I don't have cranks round me, Raccamond.
Listen, there's only one rule in business. Anyone's money is good.
That's my rule. When money walks in the door, takes off its hat and
says, 'Here I am: I want to live with you,' the least of the polite things

you can do, is to say, 'Good day; take a seat.' How else are we to get business? You're crazy if you're waiting for clean money. Did you ever hear of clean money?" (p. 309)

And, finally, William on Jules, who in the bank's crisis has broken his promise not to gamble on the Paris market:

"Of course, Jules doesn't know how to tell the truth; he doesn't know what it is. I don't think he knows his own name. He lies about it to himself at night. My name's Evarist Zugger, or let's say, Peter Mugger or better Timothy Hugger: I have twenty million francs, or 150,000,000 francs; I've sold short eighty-five thousand shares yesterday and two million today, that makes a handful of fireworks! What a splendid firebug I am! I'm a genius and my name is Aristide Scarface, I'm a *nervi* from Marseille, I'm Popoff the anarchist, I'm getting the White Russians on Tardieu's payroll, what a smart fellow I am! That's Jules's conversation with himself at night. An eagle of finance who only lays duck eggs, and who doesn't know whether he's a mocking bird or a vulture." (p. 581)

It is this kind of rhetoric which has taken over from the more formalized poetic monologue discussed in Chapter 2. Occasionally it runs into set speeches of great length where matters of central concern are being elaborated, as in the tremendous denunciation of the money grubbers by Adam Constant, teller, poet, and Communist in *Scene Eight*, "J'Accuse." This might be taken to include a statement of Christina Stead's purpose (or part of it) in writing *House of All Nations.*

"There are no men in this bank," remarked Constant, "only money galls of one color and another shape: only an infection of monsters with purses at their waists that we wait upon and serve. . . . My dream is, that one day I will get them all down, I will leave them on record." (p. 80)

Constant's attack has the cumulative force of a Shavian tirade.

XII   *Alphendéry's Role*

We should not identify the author with Constant. Adam's is one view, a perfectly intelligible one, of an actor involved in the drama. Alphendéry, on the other hand, though also an actor in the same drama, is clearly more detached emotionally than Constant and, as befits his role, a more reliable critic and commentator. It is to Alphendéry that we must look (perhaps because he himself is caught in an ambiguous moral position) for the book's ethical center.

As a socialist Alphendéry is, of course, opposed to the sordid and soulless business of private profiteering and sympathetic toward Constant and Jean Frère, the Communist writer and idealist. It never ceases to amaze Jules that Alphendéry should be so much more concerned with making money for the bank than for himself. Alphendéry could do with more money, for he has a divorced wife and an aging mother to think of. Accordingly, when Jules does bring off a big coup he makes Alphendéry a handsome gift. But the opportunities that lie to hand do not even tempt Michel. As he says to Jules: " 'You see, I'm not preaching humanity to you. You have to be born to love of humanity, and trained to it, the way you have to be born to money love' " (p. 198).

When times get bad Alphendéry urges Jules to cut free, pay his creditors (to Jules a monstrous suggestion) and set up with him and William in some more reputable enterprise where they could still make money with their knowledge and wits. Alphendéry's principles, based on personal and social responsibility, are clear and honorable, yet he does to some extent compromise them simply by working for a private bank which must help to perpetuate the system of capitalism. Furthermore, though he has scruples and Jules none, Alphendéry (for reasons of loyalty, affection and even pure fun) is prepared to tag along with many of the bank's doubtful practices.[12] Still, though he enjoys the work and some of the trickery that goes on, he is well aware of his dilemma. He would sooner be elsewhere and when matters get worse he keeps on pleading with Jules to release him. When Jules asks him why he is in this game Alphendéry says it is because he cannot abandon his dependents to poverty for the sake of his principles and because, in the tradition of his family, he has been in finance since he was a boy. When his father died he became the secretary of an Alsatian millionaire, a pro-Dreyfusite and Marxist. So Michel became a fervent Marxist too. " 'You see, I have always been a revolutionary at ease, the shadow of a rich man. It would take a violent effort of will to wrench myself out of that setting, and I suppose I will some day. If I go round much longer with Jean Frère I certainly will'" (p. 353). As it happens Alphendéry ends up with Léon—another compromise.

Alphendéry is not only a lucid expounder of technical problems but also a skilful campaigner, as his brilliant performance in court against the pompous fools Rosenkrantz and Guildenstern demonstrates (*Scene Seventy-five*). He tells Stewart, a London broker, all for Christianity and the Empire, that he favors "socialist organization" and, spurred on by Stewart's obtuseness, adds "'I mean a revolution to wipe us all out, all of us who scrounge on others and ravage the wealth of the world—you and Jules Bertillon and me. We must all go'" (p. 328). But in his calmer moments he knows the millennium is not just around the corner.

Alphendéry has a sense of history and this makes his the most comprehensive vision in the book. As early as *Scene Two* he expresses the notion, which the rest of the action is by implication to confirm, that life goes on whatever the corruption that surrounds it, that money-making organizations constitute one of the realities underlying social change, and, indeed, that revolution itself produces new markets. It is this sort of observation that makes *House of All Nations* more than an indictment of capitalism. Alphendéry is, in fact, an exception to the remark about economists made by Oliver Fenton in one of his rare moments of insight.

"Most of our economists, even our best theoretical Marxians . . . even those who write most intelligently about politics and human nature, write irritating polemic platitudes when it comes to business, because they have never been in it. Business-men are not mannequins of the class war, and individual businesses are not patterns of the decline of capitalism." [13]

XIII   *Léon and Raccamond*

Though possessed by the same mania as Jules, both Léon and Raccamond are entirely different personalities from him and from each other. The crude, swaggering Léon domineering and impetuous, exudes vitality. Alphendéry comes to admire him for his quick wits, and the knowledge and skill with which he conducts his business, qualities largely obscured by Léon's meanness in small things, his bewildering, disjointed speech and the almost incredible naïvety of his courting of women. Léon is, in fact, a good judge of character; he appreciates Alphendéry's worth, and quickly sums up the weaknesses of both Jules and Raccamond. He is one of those fictional characters who seem to embody some natural force that guarantees the appropriateness of what they do and say.[14] Not the least of Christina Stead's achievements here is the way Léon becomes, irresistibly, one of the most attractive characters in the whole book. He does not improve morally (that is not the point), but he grows on the reader, for all his roguery, crudity, and boisterousness, as a figure rendered with an artistic sympathy and understanding. He comes through more successfully than his counterpart Robbie Grant of *A Little Tea, a Little Chat,* partly because the characterization conveys this sense of creative delight and partly because, unlike Grant, he is not on stage all the time and so his antics do not become tiresome.

Aristide Raccamond is the fourth of this notable group of large-scale portraits and further proof of Christina Stead's advance in powers of characterization by the time she came to write *House of All Nations.* Once again the character is seen in the round with that artistic objectivity which blends detachment and sympathy. A most unattractive fellow in many ways, a spy and a flatterer, a craven always ready to throw blame on others, an ambitious man who lacks the unashamed drive and the ruthless calculation of his wife Marianne, and who needs her to urge him on, petty and vindictive when he gets the upper hand, Raccamond is still no monster. He is a neurotic who wants rewards for his more or less honest labors, who feels an acute responsibility for the clients who have entrusted their money to him, and who is aghast to learn the extent to which Jules's banking practice affronts conventional morality. The paradox about Raccamond is that, though his behavior is to the contrary, he sincerely believes that there is more to life than money. In a moment of genuine bewilderment he confesses as much to Marianne, but her task is always to win him to the opposite point of view. She is the clear-headed and single-minded one. Raccamond's better feelings contribute to his downfall. He becomes ludicrous and repellent at the end but this is caused by his becoming practically insane with worry, fear, and frustration as he sees his life's work crumbling and all the chances of getting control of the Banque Mercure slipping away. A tougher, self-disciplined man could have won others to stand by his just causes. It is typical of Raccamond that he should believe Alphendéry, the Jew, is the evil genius behind the bank, whereas Alphendéry is more honest than most and has always taken Raccamond's part in arguments with Jules. It is typical of Alphendéry that, on learning Raccamond has stolen the Brussels books, he should say: "'I don't think he's a real blackmailer. . . . I think he's terribly startled at what he's found out'" (p. 645).[15] It is the mixture of Raccamond's motives that gives force and conviction to his frantic behavior in the final stages of the story.

Raccamond is most appropriately named; he brings ruin to the bank. Jules looks upon him as an evil omen from the start. Raccamond even boasts of his destructive power when he is putting the pressure on Jules: "'Raccamond. . . . think of the name: it's going to be synonymous with ruin'" (p. 715). Indeed, names often signify character in *House of All Nations*. Jules is associated with the Banque Mercure, and as an actor says: "'Bertillon is altogether the personage of the old-world Mercury!'" (p. 598). Jules's toady Bomba is full of bombast, and the names Rosencrantz and Guildenstern, Constant and Frère, speak for themselves. Since Michel's surname is taken, presumably, from the millionaire whose secretary he becomes, it is perhaps not too fanciful to say that it suggests he is living an assumed role—certainly he regards his job as a form of slavery and feels his basic allegiance is to Frère rather than to Jules.

XIV *Style*

An American reviewer praised *House of All Nations* as a masterpiece which in its savage satire of "the principle of money" brings up to date the theme of Balzac's *La Comédie Humaine*.[16] Not all the reviewers approved: one Australian critic parroted Barnard Eldershaw's "rich and strange" to describe its style—a manifest absurdity because there is nothing in the writing here that is at all comparable to the exotic and luxuriant qualities that Barnard Eldershaw found in the earlier books.[17] The style of *House of All Nations* is far more disciplined and matter-of-fact; it is scored by a sharp and often savage wit and irony, as befits the tough-mindedness that lies behind it. Its characteristic bite is suggested by this description of Stewart:

An English broker visiting Jules Bertillon both for personal and bank business, cool as a cucumber, in appearance like a gray, superfine badger bristle in a Piccadilly shaving brush, seeming to despise faintly

but wholesomely the excitable Gaul, bared his small red lips over his
rat teeth and passed upstairs. (p. 235)

Or this of the employee in one of the tellers' cubicles:

In the first of these, seated on a high chair, her rosy beauty always
framed in that green air, strange behind gilt bars, like a madonna
materialized in prison, sat the customers' mail girl, Mlle. Armelle
Paëz. She watched and meditated, smiled and got invitations to dinner from all the high-stepping male clients. (p. 108)

William's speech accords with the general tone of the book. His
brand of ironical poetry is often evoked by the exasperating behavior of Jules:

"I hope he'll come to his senses after this: instead of spending his life
with idiotic playboys. So there they are: Prince Jules in a private suite,
Claire-Josèphe engaging nurses and bringing surgeons from Paris,
Bomba blowing his own kazoo on a platform of gold, Raccamond
that great jelly and his Diana-wife hunting in open season on our
preserves." (p. 461)

Finally here is William, irritably, to Raccamond:

"What do you want now? You've gouged our eyes out, slit our ears,
bit our noses, sold our tripes for cat's meat: what else? We've only got
our underwear." (p. 711)

XV Length and Scope

The Australian critic referred to above also complains that
Christina Stead "allows herself to be preoccupied and side-
tracked by an infinite variety of queer characters and incidents
intensely interesting in themselves, no doubt, but distracting to
the reader who seeks, in vain, a stable thread which might lead
him out of the maze." [18] It is not true that *House of All Nations* is
a confusing book—it has a firm theme and a clear narrative line,
and the collapse of the bank (toward which the whole book
moves from the start with Raccamond operating in the very first
scene) is obviously the "comprehensible climax" that this critic
was unable to find. This remark does, however, raise the question
of the book's length and scope. Here personal responses will vary,

but some comparisons may help to put the matter into perspective.

House of All Nations is a long and densely packed novel, built on the same scale as, say *Pendennis* and *Bleak House*, which did not seem too long to Victorian readers. It is shorter than some of the best-sellers of the twentieth century, for example, *Anthony Adverse* and *Gone with the Wind*. It is certainly an easier book to read and absorb than *The Ambassadors*, or *Ulysses*, or the much shorter *The Sound and the Fury*, all of which have attained the status of modern classics. It has an intensity that some readers would, no doubt, find disturbing; the novelist has seen so much to support the view of life that she presents and she wants to include all the evidence. *House of All Nations* is one of those novels which hammer away obsessively at their themes. It is money, money, money on every page, just as in Richardson's *Clarissa* (a far longer book) it is sex, sex, sex; perhaps novelists really possessed by their subjects are bound to write long books. Christina Stead happens to be this kind of writer—the deeply committed, concentrating, obsessive. And it is this that accounts for the most powerful of her effects in books like *House of All Nations, For Love Alone*, and *The Man Who Loved Children*.

If *House of All Nations* is too long it is because of the hosts of minor figures who swarm over its pages. It is such a rich book, so full of observation and invention that superfluity is a price that has to be paid. Sometimes the characters develop away from the initial sketch given of them. A minor instance of this occurs with Carrière—of some significance, perhaps, as he is the least convincing of the main characters. When he first appears Carrière is described as a "dumpy, red-haired young man." A few scenes later he still has the same arrogant look that is specified in the first description but is now tall and blond. More important, because it seems to show a character taking over from the author, is the case of Davigdor Schicklgrüber, the ugly blond lout, stalking-horse for Lord Zinovraud, the multimillionaire. The main point about Schicklgrüber is that his apparent stupidity and brutality is probably a cloak for his shrewdness and an aid in collecting women and valuable business information for his master. So we are told, when he first appears, "Davidgor had a vocabulary of two or three hundred words at the most and a lot of those were primitive Anglo-Saxon, also common in low German" (p. 372). And his early speech endorses this description. But within two or three pages Schicklgrüber is talking almost as eloquently as the Bertillons or Alphendéry:

"Jules, go the right way about it. For instance, you're going to have trouble with this louse Carrière. This self-decorated Christmas tree Carrière has got the first infirmity of feeble minds. He's telling it round that he's going to buy a newspaper. Now, you keep away from all that and you'll win hands down. Never own a newspaper; own journalists: never buy the news-services. Just pay a whisper: never involve a politician—he'll let you down or be let out. And compromise: don't fight." (pp. 375–76)

It might be argued that Jules himself gets out of hand occasionally. When in a good mood he has an infectious sense of humor which is always running off into fantasy. In a discussion as to the advisability of closing down the bank (a favorite topic) Jules prattles on:

"We'll scatter and then we'll meet again at a fixed place on a fixed date. We can fly. William still has a pilot's license. Alphendéry gets air-sick but he's necessary because he can hand out the flapdoodle to passport officials and he looks like a Bulgarian or a Spaniard or something. By the way, Michel. Your friends down in the Communist Party must know a lot about faking passports. Why don't you go down and get us a wad of false passports, for Claire and the boys and the twins and William, you, and me." (p. 211)

Here he is simply enjoying himself and the passage is in character. So too are the hilariously fantastic plans for making money that he talks about in Scene Forty-seven; smuggling tobacco into France through naval submarine officers, flooding the market with a new peach brandy, and reviving Monte Carlo by means of a bargain between Jews and the Pope—financial returns in exchange for a Papal bull making divorce easy in the municipality. There seems no limit to his gaiety and inventiveness. But what are we to make of the vicious schemes he puts forward in Scene Forty-six for buying up land in some poor country and going to live among the peasants in order to exploit them in truly medieval fashion? Here Jules is said to be in earnest but, even allowing that he is supposed to be an admirer of all kinds of money-makers, the tone (at least) of these speeches seems to jar. It is as if he is being forced into a more villainous role than he deserves.[19]

Despite such inconsistencies, *House of All Nations* is an impressive book. Perhaps the finest of its scenes is "The Stuffed Carp," which for devastating irony and mordant comedy is unsurpassed by anything else Christina Stead has ever written.

XVI   An Ironic Masterpiece: "The Stuffed Carp"

This magnificent scene describes one of the regular dinner visits paid by the Raccamonds to the Hallers, rich clients of Aristide's with an obsession about property of all kinds and about food. Although Haller has not yet brought him much business, Raccamond cannot afford to neglect such a customer and so he regularly comes along to endure the monstrous feasts Madame Haller loves to prepare. The entertaining of the Raccamonds does not spring from friendship or liberality; it is an occasion Haller uses to air his opinions on public affairs and to drain Aristide of useful financial information, and Madame Haller to extract envy and flattery from her less fortunate guests. In her hands, especially, the dinner party becomes an act of tyranny masked by sweetness, a form of display and an occasion for domination. She has piles of priceless possessions, which she can never bear to use, hoarded away—exquisite linen and slips, embroidery and hand-made lace purchased from humble women who have given years and their eyesight to its creation, carpets, curtains, shawls and robes. These and their valuable furniture, which is stored away in case war or revolution should suddenly break out in Europe, are investments more solid than gold.

Madame Haller forces massive quantities of food upon the sycophantic Raccamonds, who are expected to praise everything extravagantly. The feast begins with servings of chicken liver washed down by glass after glass of Cointreau. Then comes the pièce de résistance, the huge stuffed carp; this, with the aid of chartreuse to stimulate the gastric juices, they manage to consume. Now comes the wine, kept for years (and so another cause for self-congratulation) and its flavor gone; this is followed by a miscellany of port, peaches and cream, nuts, sugar, butter, chocolates and honey. Haller at this point starts cheerfully on sausage and Burgundy, and Aristide, protesting, has to follow suit. Tortured by indigestion, green and gasping for breath, Raccamond strug-

gles to the window and stages a partial recovery, only to return to
the fray and find tea being served with the chocolates. Madame
Haller manages finally to force a splendid Doyenne de Comice
pear upon Aristide, specially bought because he needs fresh fruit
for his digestion.

Two strands of conversation weave their way through this pro-
miscuous guzzling and gorging. There is Madame Haller's continual fuss about the purity of the food they eat—only one special
brand of tinned peaches, a specially prepared butter sent by a
country producer, and so on. The other strand concerns Europe
and financial matters, talk that provides a counterpointed comment to the feast. Apparently unaware of the implications, Haller
can say:

"Nothing arouses hate for the ruling classes like excessive taxes and
an excessive burden of internal debt. Lenin saw this. He acted as a
cathartic; the ruling classes in Russia had stuffed themselves to
bursting on interest. You see, the financial papers enable the people
to see the Fat People eating."

Raccamond asks, " 'You mean the financiers?' " and Haller goes
on:

"Yes I call them the Fat People. Now, human nature teaches us, we
know by instinct, that there is something wrong when five per cent of
the people stuff and ninety-five per cent have almost nothing to eat
and no money to put into interest-bearing bonds at all." (p. 289)

The Hallers are aghast to learn that their guests love a *pâté de
foie gras* which they get in tins from the Dordogne—tinned food
is bad enough (when others buy it), but don't they know that
pâté is made from the diseased livers of overfed geese? The Hallers could not possibly eat it.

Food is the metaphor of this scene. This account of a dinner
party is a far more effective denunciation of acquisitiveness and
greed, of self-indulgence and hypocrisy, of servility and self-
righteousness, than a whole volume of sermons. Fielding often
uses similar imagery for satiric as well as purely humorous purposes, but the substance and tone of "A Stuffed Carp" is closer
to Swift's "A Modest Proposal." [20] The title is especially appropri-

ate—the carp is omnivorous and so are the people who stuff themselves with food like this. And the reader is free to follow the
secondary implications if he cares to.[21]

The experience of the evening leads Marianne to reflect upon
money as she and Aristide are on their way home.

"There's no subject so rich in ideas as Money." Aristide grunted.
"I'm thinking," went on Marianne tenderly, with a richer tone than
she usually used, "that money is a very pure thing in its way; that's
why the Hallers have such curious habits. They have nothing more to
do, they do not even need more money—they have enough for
avarice. Now they are looking for the absolute. They caught that
from their gold bars. It is an absolute. People have such a delicate
love for money that if you speak jealously of it or of those who own it,
all the dirt falls back on you: people take you for a miserable, poor-
spirited person." (p. 300)

This is a key passage in the book and it confirms the view of
House of All Nations as a twentieth-century version of the search
for the absolute—a theme made memorable by Balzac in his story
of Balthazar Claes (*La Recherche de l'Absolu*), who in his zeal to
discover the philosopher's stone destroys himself and brings ruin
upon his family. In *Scene Seventeen,* one of the few occasions
where the author directly addresses the reader, the same idea is
explored and this conclusion is reached: "In the old days those
that sought the absolute tried to make gold: our own conception
is not very different" (p. 136).

CHAPTER 4

Love, Hate, and Marriage

THE next two books, *The Man Who Loved Children* and *For Love Alone*, mark the peak of Christina Stead's achievement to date and must occupy high places in any ranking of novels by Australian writers. The first, as more and more critics of discernment are coming to realize, is a masterpiece which will outlive much of the highly praised fiction of our time, and the second is not so far behind it in quality. We move now from the public world of international finance and the social panorama of *House of All Nations* to the narrower, more intensely focused pictures of individuals struggling toward self-realization, and of family life.

Virginia Woolf admitted her failure to solve the problem of telling the truth about her own experiences "as a body." Her readers will agree—even the most closely and sympathetically studied of her women characters seem the products of a refined and overanxious sensibility that drains them of physical vitality. Christina Stead's women are different. Henrietta suffers all the torments of a passionate woman caught in a disastrous marriage (despite her large family she seeks the solace of a lover) and Teresa, for all her spiritual intensities, is also a creature of the flesh, as her rescue from the streets by Quick and the final intriguing sequences of *For Love Alone* prove. Realizing what Miss Haviland has suffered at the hands of Jonathan Crow, Teresa at one point says she wants to write a novel about the sorrows of women; later this idea gives way to a project called " 'The Seven Houses of Love,' . . . the ages, a sacred seven, through which abandoned, unloved women passed before life was torn out of their clenched, ringless, workworn fists, a story of these days, perhaps of yours" (p. 419).

Toward the end of *The Man Who Loved Children* Henny (as she is usually called), throwing aside a "saga of upland Georgian gentility" which for the fourth time she has failed to read, says, " 'I'm a failure all right, . . . and why don't they write about

deadbeats like me—only it wouldn't sell!'"[1] Teresa shares with
Henny (and Louisa) "the natural outlawry of womankind." Both
suffer from the men who enslave them. Henny is doomed to defeat but Teresa breaks free before the situation closes round her.

In these two novels Christina Stead writes of individuals whose
struggles and sufferings come to represent if not those of women
in general then those of many women. After his wife's death there
is public sympathy for Sam as the injured party—the irony of this
suggests that things are never likely to be any different for the
Henriettas in this world. At the end of *For Love Alone* Teresa can
scarcely believe that she ever loved or imagined she loved Jonathan, and she reflects, "'It's dreadful to think that it will go on
being repeated for ever, he—and me! What's there to stop it?'"
(p. 502). Teresa becomes the heroine of a book similar in kind to
the one she wanted to write. *The Man Who Loved Children* goes
to prove that novelists occasionally write about "deadbeats" like
Henny, whether such books turn out to be best-sellers or not.

I   The Man Who Loved Children: *Setting and Story*

There is a thematic continuity between these novels. *The Man
Who Loved Children* ends with Louisa, having broken from the
family, at the beginning of her voyage into the outer world, where
the future awaits the budding writer. The Ulysses theme of *For
Love Alone* takes shape in Teresa's voyages. She, like Louisa, lives
in a family from which she must escape; older and less dependent
she finds freedom (or at least the first steps toward it) easier to
seek. Harper's Ferry becomes the symbolic goal in each book. It is
the beauty spot in wild country beyond her aunt's cottage at
Narara where Teresa decides to go, when she walks out of her
teaching job; she does not reach her destination, but it is her first
real journey alone and from then on she turns her eyes toward
Europe and the voyage she is ultimately to achieve. Harper's
Ferry is the place, up country again, owned by Louisa's relatives,
where she has stayed in summer vacations; at the end of *The Man
Who Loved Children* Louisa sets out for Harper's Ferry—significantly, on her own , not with her school friend Clare who, when
put to the test, is afraid to accompany her. *The Man Who Loved
Children* and *For Love Alone*, in fact, draw together a number of
basic, recurring subjects, all of which are either handled or foreshadowed in *Seven Poor Men of Sydney*—the tensions of family

life, rebellious youth, the search for love and freedom, the stir-
rings of artistic impulse, and the dilemmas of womankind. These
are topics close to the writer's heart and it is this deep emotional
involvement, combined with maturity of judgment, that contributes so much to the success of these two novels.

Though on first reading *The Man Who Loved Children* seems
to be dominated by Sam Pollit (such is the power with which he
is presented), it is essentially a novel about a family, in which the
wife and eldest child play roles that are, in the final analysis, as
important as the father's. Samuel Clemens Pollit (note the Mark
Twain flavor of the name) lives with his family in Tohoga House,
a mansion set amid large grounds in Georgetown, D.C. His wife
Henrietta is from the well-to-do Collyer family in Baltimore; the
eldest child is Louisa (the only child of Sam's by his first wife,
now dead) eleven and a half years old, fat, overgrown, and unattractive. The children of Sam's marriage to Henrietta are Ernest
aged ten (Henny's favorite), a friendly lad with an abiding but
unselfish interest in money, Evie aged eight (Sam's favorite), Saul
and Samuel the seven-year-old twins, and Tommy aged four. During the course of the story yet another child is born to Henny,
named (by Sam) Charles Franklin—Charles after his grandfather
and Franklin after one of Sam's idols, F. D. Roosevelt, whom he
regards as the first great socialist ruler. With the family lives Sam's
younger sister Bonnie, who acts as a general servant in the household.

Henny, used to comfort and money, has married "a mere jog-
trot subaltern bureaucrat" without a university degree, who owes
his job as a naturalist in the Conservation Bureau to her father's
influence. Sam never had money; indeed, he is proud of the fact
that he is a bricklayer's son, who left school at the age of twelve
and has made his way into what he likes to believe is an important
national position. Sam fancies himself even more than usual when
he is appointed to an Anthropological Mission that is to go to the
Pacific. He is, in his own eyes, a saintly moralist, in love with the
world, but who, unfortunately, has chosen a woman who (now, at
least) hates him. Henny and Sam are opposite in temperament
and inhabit different worlds—hers sharp, nasty but individual; his
moral, high-minded, and abstract. Sam could be vile, but in joke;
Henny was "beautifully, wholeheartedly vile." Henny is a bad

manager and perpetually short of money. Sam, "the man who loves children" as she calls him derisively in one of their many bitter quarels, spends most of his time playing and playing at working with them and seems not to care about Henny's difficulties, or even the bread-and-butter demands of a large family. Yet beneath all the hatred there remain, as Sam says in one of his more attractive moments, some vestiges of love:

For a moment, after years of scamping, she felt the dread power of wifehood; they were locked in each other's grasp till the end—the end, a mouthful of sunless muckworms and grass roots stifling his blare of trumpets and her blasphemies against love. The timid, fame-loving wretch would never dare to shake her off; and that was how she had him still. (p. 145)

The story traces the course of the bitter, destructive feuding between husband and wife, the children becoming both subjects and allies in the struggle. Henny keeps threatening to leave Sam and take the children with her but he, who likes to think of himself as a good family man, insists that the children come first, and that the home must not be broken up. As the eldest, Louisa is best able to understand what is going on and with unobtrusive skill Christina Stead manages to bring her more and more toward the center of the book as she grows into adolescence and the psychological relationships among the three main characters increase in complexity.

The first two chapters establish the family situation and describe in detail Sam's philosophy of life and his everlasting horseplay with the children, himself the chief humorist and, of course, the big boss. Chapter 3 focuses attention on Louisa and Henny, whose lover is the good-natured Bert Anderson, a man sorry for her rather than deeply in love with her. The next chapter describes the gradual development of one of Sam and Henny's terrible quarrels, which reaches its climax when she hurls hysterical abuse at him, he hits her, and she wounds him with a knife. This chapter ends with a most beautifully calculated and deeply moving scene in which Henny, her rage all spent and ashamed of drawing his blood, submits (but defensively, in a wryly ironical manner) to his pleas for a renewal of their love and the pledge of another child, before he leaves on his trip overseas.

She started up, trembling; but his long fidelity to her, of which she felt sure, moved her beyond all her resolutions. She began to gather up the cups and saucers and, to justify herself, she thought, "I'll wring every penny of my debts out of him some way, before he goes; I'll find a way, anyway. I won't suffer," and a small trickle of courage came back into her veins. (p. 149)

We learn, casually, later on that Henny in fact gets her own way over Hazel Moore. (It is disagreement about her that sparks off the long quarrel in Chapter 4.) In its compassion, unmarred by sentimentality or false pathos, and its profound understanding of human suffering and desire, this account of a temporary reconciliation unexpectedly achieved when the antagonists are momentarily lifted out of and above their normal selves, is fine enough to stand by the magnificent scene in *Anna Karenina* where Vronsky and Alexei Karenin are reconciled, as it seems that Anna is about to die. Chapter 5 describes a visit by Henny and Louisa to the Collyer's family home, Monocacy, and Chapter 6 shows us Sam in Malaya, with the anthropological expedition, loving all his black and yellow brothers and spreading the gospel of peace and enlightenment.

After eight months' absence Sam returns home to a big welcome from all the Pollit clan. The celebrations are interrupted by another of Henny's abusive displays, which hastens the birth of her child. Henny's father has just died and Sam hopes that Tohoga House will now become his property, but in the settlement of the estate it is sold and Henny inherits nothing substantial. At this point Sam's fortunes begin to decline at work also; scandals circulate about Henny's baby and with the death of David Collyer, Sam loses support and is to be eased out of the Conservation Bureau. Characteristically, he believes that good will triumph and he refuses to answer the charges brought against him. The family moves into a broken-down old place, Spa House, by a creek in a decayed part of Annapolis. Sam has by now been suspended from work and the only money coming into the household is Henny's meager quarterly allowance from her father's estate. Sam seems as happy as ever, busy with the children, patching up the house, spouting his ideals and organizing his little community around him.

Henny is by this time in complete despair; the antagonisms

deepen, and Louisa begins to rebel against her father's interference in her private life and his attempts to win her to his side in the fight against Henny. By Chapter 9 Henny has given up all her pretensions to middle-class elegance and gets away from the home as often as she can. At the same time it is clear that Sam is beginning to lose his hold over Ernie as well as Louisa, who is now passionately fond of her teacher Miss Aiden. In desperation one day Henny goes to Washington hoping for help from Bert Anderson, but once he hears of the scandal and an anonymous letter Sam has received he immediately breaks off the relationship. Bert, it should be added, works in the Department of Internal Revenue and fears for his position.

The final long chapter brings Henny's worsening plight to its inevitable end. She returns home after three days (during which time she has vainly hoped Sam might start divorce proceedings) to learn that Bonnie, who had disappeared some time before, has turned up at the boardinghouse owned by Josephine, Sam's sister, to have a baby. Henny's last days are lived amid the terrible stench of oil that Sam and the children are collecting from the boiling down of a marlin—yet another of his crazy experimental games which he justifies as an economy measure. The conflicts between Sam and Henny mount, ending in a physical struggle in which Henny, now practically insane, threatens to kill herself and the rest of the family.

Louisa, feeling the responsibility thrown upon her in this crisis, decides to do away with both parents to save herself and the other children. She is firmly convinced of the rightness of her plans and just trusts to luck that she will not be suspected in the enquiry that must follow into their deaths. Put to the test she falters and succeeds in placing the poison in one cup of tea only. Henny has observed her guilty behavior, guesses what she has done, and deliberately drinks the tea as a way out of an impossible situation. Sam, of course, is only too ready to believe that Henny has planned her own suicide. We note here the strict honesty of Christina Stead's handling of Louisa throughout this sequence of events. Louisa quickly adopts Sam's explanation of suicide in order to protect herself. The extent of Henny's debts comes out at the coroner's enquiry and Sam, on whom so much of the blame really rests, is eager to play the part of the upright and deceived husband, who will exert himself to pay all debts and clear the family name. He can now welcome Bonnie and her baby to the home and look forward to the pleasures of bringing up yet another child. Louisa, finally, can endure his smugness and self-deception no longer and in a last attempt to force him to face reality tells him the whole truth about her plans to kill both parents. Sam, characteristically, refuses to believe her and the next morning Louisa leaves home and takes the road to Harper's Ferry.

II Sam: The Individual and Representative Character

The most striking thing about *The Man Who Loved Children* is the character of Sam Pollit and all that he so unforgettably represents. "Represents" must be emphasized, for Sam is one of those rare fictional characters who is big enough and, in presentation, strong enough to stand for a whole way of life. And this he does, because like all truly representative characters, he is (paradoxical as it may seem) thoroughly individual as well. In an early review N. L. Rothman said that Pollitry ought to achieve the notoriety of Babbittry—a fair statement, because Sam is as memorable as Babbitt. He can be variously described because, though unspared in the presentation, he is not just a cardboard figure set up as a target for satire. He is a genuine, if naïve, optimist, and a mealy-mouthed idealist who believes that the world can be saved by science and socialism; he is upright and honest and faithful to his wife, yet he destroys her and corrupts the family more surely than most less moral men would be capable of doing, so that she can say, " 'Why with his prudery and chastity the wretch has used me up more than four husbands' " (p. 138).

Sam is fond of his children and, while they are young, provides them endlessly with exciting activities, workgames, and funny stories interspersed with instructive orations, but he must always be the biggest child in the band, the constant center of attention and admiration—a coaxing, wheedling, facetious tyrant who becomes nasty and querulous once he fails to get his own way. All his spare time he spends with the children creating a kind of phoney kindergarten atmosphere designed to amuse and instruct according to the latest and most enlightened educational theory, a theory which nevertheless makes the onlooker suspect a basic falsity in this relation between old and young. Each child has to await a special whistle summoning him or her to meals; there is also a special whistle for sitting down and all must wait outside the dining room until it is given.

He has nicknames for them all (and for certain adults too)—Looloo (Loobyloo, Loogoobrious, Bluebeak etc.), Bonniferous, Sawbones, Little Womey (woman) for his favorite Evie. He prattles away continually in his special blend of baby talk. Artemus Ward jocosities, and Uncle Remus dialect: "'Bring up your tea, Looloo-girl: I'm sick, hot head, nedache [headache], dot pagans in my stumjack [got pains in my stomach]: want my little fambly around me this morning'" (p. 30), though he is quick to drop it when he feels his audience beginning to resist his wiles. Sam, of course is a non-drinker and non-smoker, and tries to instil his beliefs, his worship of science, and his hatred of religion into the children. He professes to believe in the natural rights of the child; yet, in the name of character building, he can force little Sam, who is sick with the stench of marlin offal, to cart it away, and even throws some of the vile stuff over the boy's head to cure him of his weakness.

Considering the time he spends with them, Sam in certain important ways is curiously ignorant of children, though he gets on better with them than with adults. He does not seem to know (or care) whether he humiliates them or not and he can show a complete disregard for their feelings. There is, for instance, the revolting scene in which he chews up a sandwich and then siphons it into Tommy's mouth, lecturing his young audience as he does so: "'Not only for the ptyalin . . . which is now already mixed with the food and helps Tommy to digest, but also for the communization of germs. Tommy will not, I think, suffer from the dyspepsia that all you other kids do'" (p. 57). Not content with this he tries to do the same to his Looloo, who breaks away from him in embarrassment. (Significantly, this incident occurs after some sentimental reminiscing about his first wife, Rachel.) To take another instance, Sam encourages an argument between Ernest and Saul, urges them to fight (in order to get rid of bad blood), but, when Saul finally runs away, leads the rest of his gang in pursuit, gleefully taunting the youngster with cowardice. It is not surprising that this is the eugenist who advocates the weeding out of misfits and degenerates, the humanitarian who in a typical lecture to Louisa justifies murder and suicide in a speech the reader will recall when he comes to the book's final scenes.

Perhaps the worst feature of Sam's relationship with his children is his interference in their lives; this incurable desire to know all their secrets is one more symptom of his egocentricity. As Louisa grows into adolescence Sam becomes obsessed with the desire to police her thoughts and feelings; he cannot resign himself to the fact that she is an individual with her own rights and is beginning to assert her independence. Sam is a Peter Pan who will not himself grow up and who does not want his children to grow up either. Such a man will obviously be a poor hand at adult relationships. In Malaya one evening after dinner he sees fit to lecture Lady Modore about superfluous hair; hair under the arms, he tells her, should never be removed; since nature put it there it must have some use. He might be Sam the Bold with the children, but in the office he is known as "soft-soap Sam" and to his wife he is "the great I-Am."

III   *Conflict between Husband and Wife*

The conflict between husband and wife dramatizes, in an extreme form, not only the division between the sexes but also the difference between two ways of life: the first, professing morality, makes a mockery of it by replacing the reality of human feelings with words, whereas the second, though immoral by conventional standards, is redeemed by its capacity for suffering and fellow-feeling. Sam and Henny are temperamental opposites, but not of the complementary kind. To the children ". . . their father was the tables of the law, but their mother was natural law; Sam was household czar by divine right, but Henny was the czar's everlasting adversary, household anarchist by divine right" (p. 34). Even in her worst moments of tiredness and despair Henny usually has the strength to resist "the depraved healthiness and jollity of the Pollit clan." Sam's relatives are not bad people but Henny just cannot endure them—she recoils as instinctively as one would from a person whose breath smells. The dark-light symbolism is now given a more precise form than it had in the poetic reverberations of *Seven Poor Men of Sydney*. It seems appropriate that Sam, the incurable optimist, should be plump, blue-eyed, and fair. "When he waved his golden-white muscular hair-

less arms, large damp tufts of yellow-red hair appeared. . . . The
pores on his well stretched skin were very large, his leathery skin
was quite unlike the dull silk of the children's cheeks" (p. 49).
The children look more like Henny, who is dark and lean with
"large, bright eyeballs, and thin, high-curved black eyebrows" and
long olive hands—a figure fit for tragedy.

Once again it is Christina Stead's imaginative grasp of character
and the richly expressive sensory detail through which the character is realized that put the stamp of authenticity on Henny. Her
exasperation with Sam drives her more and more to seek the solitude of her room, there to play solitaire, wash down aspirin with
black tea and eat the sharp-flavored foods that Sam, the health
faddist, shudders at—toast, pickles, cold meat, curry, gherkins,
chilies and Worcestershire sauce. Worn out by children, the drudg-
ery of housework, shortage of money and mounting debts, Henny
is the woman enslaved by marriage. Understandably (but not
altogether justly) she blames all her troubles upon Sam and, as
the book opens, their marriage has already reached the point
where they talk to each other only to quarrel. From the start the
reader senses that Henny's is a losing battle, for nothing, finally,
can shake the monumental self-assurance of Sam. Henny, unlike
him, is honest enough with herself to be capable of losing her self-
respect and this is one reason why all her raging can never completely alienate us. We understand the need that drives her into
the affair with Bert Anderson and despite her brusqueness with
the children we are made to feel the affection that lies deep in her
and in them.

The basic relationship between mother and child, that which
endures all the discords, the abuse, and the fretfulness that family
life breeds, is touched off faultlessly again and again with the min-
imum of effort. Here is an instance where every phase tells, every
detail is perfectly apt. Ernie, characteristically, is thinking about
money.

Father and Mother fought because there was not enough money
forthcoming. Mother wasted her money, and Sam was unable to
understand how expenses could be so large. If there were only
two children, himself and Louie, they would live in clover, but there
were six. What if another ever came? That would be difficult. One
morning, after thinking about this in bed, Ernie had gone to his
Mother and said, "Mothering, don't have another baby!"

Henny had said, "You can bet your bottom dollar on that, old sweetness."

Ernie did not like this feverish phrase of Henny's, for the idea of his bottom dollar ever coming to light at all (from under the heap of other dollars) did not appeal to him.

"We must never think about money," said both Auntie Jo and Daddy. Ernie knew that this was one of the pious precepts handed down by people in power to smaller people in subjection, since both Auntie Jo and Samuel constantly thought about bills, salaries, and getting on, and always had money in their purses. Ernie knew that parents and guardians handed down many other wise saws for the same purpose, which was to prevent the young ones from getting into their game too soon. (pp. 109–10)

We sense the affection behind Henny's wry "old sweetness," observe the unintended shock her words give Ernest and are then quickly back into his reflections again. It is characteristic of the close texture of *The Man Who Loved Children* that all the threads of this short scene are woven into the general fabric. The end of this chapter (where she unexpectedly submits to Sam) subjects Henny's reassuring remark to the pressure of dramatic irony, and Ernie's fears for his bottom dollar turn out to be well grounded after all. Henny's relationship with Ernest, the young financier, has that blend of delicacy and power which characterizes so many of the pages of this superb book. It would be hard to exaggerate the dramatic force and relevance of two scenes between them in Chapter 9. The first is the occasion on which Ernest discovers that his mother has sold all her most treasured private possessions (clothes, jewellery and brushes, which he loved to handle) and, worse still, has raided his cache and replaced the money with useless old foreign coins. Ernest is heartbroken by this violation and deception. Henny is conscience-stricken and promises to repay him but the damage is irreparable and she knows it.

The second, a scene of almost unbearable horror, because of the bond which we know unites them, occurs later when Ernest appears before Henny one morning in a dirty shirt, ready for school. She has only just gone through a wild hysterical scene with Sam over Louisa, who unwittingly seems to drive Henny to fury, and she immediately rushes at Ernest and beats him again and again across the head. Ernest's world is now collapsing around him; be-

wildered by the injustice of it all he does not even try to protect
himself but simply falls to his knees and repeats the word
"Mother" over and over again, pleading with her to stop. It is no
wonder that Henny is soon to welcome death, when in life she
finds herself capable of treating in this manner the one she loves
most.

Sam and Henny provide the contrast on which the book is built.
He believes in the perfectibility of man and all the humanist virtues, but his limitations as a human being are crippling, as the
following passage shrewdly indicates. "For Sam was naturally
lighthearted, pleasant, all generous effusion and responsive emo-
tion. He was incapable of nursing an injustice which would cost
him good living to repay, or evil thought which it would undo him
to give back, or even sorrow in his bosom; and tragedy itself could
not worm its way by any means into his heart. Such a thing would
have made him ill or mad, and he was all for health, sanity, success, and human love" (p. 47). Henny, on the other hand, only
too well aware of the insecurity and injustice of existence, seems
made for tragedy and this gives a touch of grandeur to her vile-
ness. The book penetrates to the reality behind the masks they
present to the world. Henny is a liar and Sam is truthful, but, as
Randall Jarrell points out, Henny is honest in her lying and Sam
dishonest in his truth. Characters with such vitality as these
could easily become caricatures but both Henny and Sam are
presented in depth.

The complexiy of the human situation as seen in *The Man Who
Loved Children* prevents us from making easy moral judgments
and simply taking her side against his. Sam is justified in expect-
ing Henny to show more affection for Louisa. He is capable of
charity, as when he supports Bonnie in her trouble—though the
critic determined to damn him might argue that Bonnie finally
confirms his complacency by bringing another child into the house
to replace defections from his infant army. But there is no reason
to suppose any insincerity in his defence of Bonnie against the
hypocritical morality of his sister Josephine. In the argument that
begins in Chapter 4 when Henny demands Hazel Moore back to
help in the house, Sam, who objects to Hazel as a Bible thumper
with a bad influence upon his children, is at first restrained and
gentle in manner. Henny here, as so often, deliberately provokes
him by her taunts and insults; she finally succeeds in making him

lose his temper by accusing him of carrying on with other women. Henny's allegations are false and she knows they are, as is made evident later on.[2] In Chapter 7 she again twists the facts by screaming in front of the Pollit clan: " 'Don't you regret my condition because of his lust? Didn't he fix me up, pin me down, make sure no man would look at me while he was gallivanting with his fine ladies?' " (p. 269). For Sam and Henny the bonds of hatred are now at least as strong as the bonds of love ever were.

In one of the relatively few passages of direct comment in this novel Christina Stead writes: "All the children, though, believed that Sam was utterly innocent, which in fact he was, innocent too, of all knowledge of men, business, and politics, a confiding and sheltered child strayed into public affairs" (pp. 334–35). This judgment is endorsed at the end by a letter written by Rachel soon after her marriage to Sam. Louisa quotes from it:

" 'Samuel is a very young man. I am very sick or I would not be writing such foolish things, I am sure. But he does not understand women or children. He is such a good young man, he is too good to understand people at all.' " (p. 524)

Christopher Ricks in a most sensitive appreciation of *The Man Who Loved Children,* says quite rightly of this passage that we underrate Sam and the book if we take it as simple irony. Ricks goes on: "Sam is a Feiffer character, but living in a fully realized world of tragedy. Not a hypocrite at all, but a classic case of the softly aggressive victim. It is all very well that the meek shall inherit the earth, but Sam, disconcertingly, seems to be doing it here and now, his other cheek turning like a top. Miss Stead catches this in five words: 'A smile bared his teeth.' "[3] "Feiffer" is meant to suggest not that Sam is merely a caricature but that as a person he differs basically from Henny. Randall Jarrell describes Sam as a character who remains his old self, who stays in the same position while Henny and Louisa move on.[4] There is, in fact, one occasion when Sam is on the threshold of a change—after his return from Malaya. Jarrell's acknowledgment of this overlooks the point that Sam's visit to the East makes him aware for the first time of other worlds both inside and outside himself. He takes joy in the porcelains, silks, and embroideries he finds there; he begins to feel there is more to life than goodness, health, science, and

progress—there is the past, the beauty of the past, and its exten-
sion into the present. He seems suddenly to have realized the
bareness of his own life; he brings home boxes of treasures, gifts
for his family; ". . . he would now be the East to his children as
well as the West" (p. 272). Before long Sam is fixed in his old
attitudes again but this interlude adds a humanizing touch and
suggests another dimension to his personality. As the gift scene
develops, our expectations are baulked by Sam's tasteless and
facetious mimicry of Louisa and her poetry. The unexpected potentialities never flower. The embryonic, serious Sam, the man
who through his love of beautiful things might have come to a
real and unselfish love of people, does not survive the death of
David Collyer, the birth of another child, and the loss of Tohoga
House.

The author's insistence on the unexpected in her major characters is a guarantee of her impartiality and of her preparedness to
face the ironies that await the patient and persistent exploration
of human behavior. The characters in *The Man Who Loved Children* possess the consistency we customarily demand in fiction and
the occasional unpredictability we need to assure us of their
uniqueness as human beings. At first it may seem incredible that
Louisa, so often the target of Henny's shameful abuse, should still
prefer Henny to Sam, who does so much to win his daughter's
love; but this is right—the unspoken bond is stronger. The reader
comes to realize, as he gets further into the book, that much of
Henny's ranting about Louisa is an outlet for the physical pain she
suffers, or a cover for her own sense of guilt and jealousy—guilt
brought about by her failure to create love and happiness out of
her marriage, and jealousy (especially in those tirades where she
dwells obsessively on the physical symptoms of adolescence) for
the incestuous element in the relationship between father and
daughter. (After all, Louisa is her stepdaughter.) Ultimately
Henny's contempt for Sam overrides everything else; she absolves
Louisa of blame as she becomes aware of the murder plot and
even admires the courage of her action. Deep down Henny knows
that Louisa has always been on her side against the Pollits.

IV   *Louisa: The Young Artist*

The remarkable thing about Louisa is that as a character she
does not suffer in comparison with such commanding figures as

Sam and Henny. The secret of Christina Stead's success here is that Louisa is a developing character whose growth is plotted against the violent constant of the husband-wife relationship. She is (to extend one of her own phrases) the talented ugly duckling who escapes—presumably into a world of swans, which for Louisa would be the community of art. *The Man Who Loved Children* spans approximately two and a half years in Louisa's life from the age of eleven and a half, but both physically and mentally Louisa is precocious and by the time the family comes to live in Spa House she looks more like fifteen. She is able to survive, more or less unscathed, on the family battlefield because of the inner security of her imaginative life. She knows she will become a writer and (as numerous critics have said) Christina Stead makes us believe too in her artistic vocation.

The budding artist is a commonplace in twentieth-century fiction—Louisa is exceptional because her story provides the evidence we need in order to confirm the promise of literary genius. Furthermore, Louisa's reading and writing are such that they express the emotional state or the spiritual crisis that she is experiencing at the time. And this appropriateness obtains whether her responses take the form of self-communings and withdrawal or of attempts to come to grip with her problems by the ceremonial act of composition. It is most fitting that Louisa should enjoy *The Cenci* once she discovers what it is really about (and ironical that Sam, who has brought her up on *The Origin of the Species* and Cuvier's *The Animal Kingdom,* should have given her Shelley, "to help her poetry") and that soon after she should compose, in a language of her own devising, a tragedy about a father who, in embracing, strangles his daughter. Its title is *Herpes Rom* or *The Snake-Man* and Sam, the man who loves reptiles as well as other forms of animal life, does not approve, even though it is her offering for his fortieth birthday enacted by Evie and Ernest. To Sam's question: Why couldn't it be in English? she counters, with all the insolence of youthful genius: " 'Did Euripides write in English?' "

V   *Political Implications*

The Man Who Loved Children is a rich book which improves with successive readings. It is, despite its concentration on a small area of life, comprehensive as well. Like all good novels its implications move ever outwards. The insight and power of its characterization are now taken for granted. Some critics have compared it to Brecht's later plays for its radical analysis of American bourgeois attitudes and illusions.[5] On its first appearance one writer said it might be considered as "a novelization of Engel's 'Origin of the Family,'" which succeeded in this "without prejudice to the integrity of the ideas or to the embodying art."[6] Others have stressed its more general political significance; the best of these statements comes from Elizabeth Hardwick, who says:

Sam Pollit's overwhelming cantish vitality is probably not a political thing in itself, but it comes from the lush underside, the slushy, rich bottom soil of the political terrain. His every sentence is a speech to his public, his family is a sort of political party to be used, fulsomely praised, and grotesquely subjected to uplifting sermons. He is literally swollen with idealistic feelings and self-love, with democratic statement and profound self-seeking.[7]

VI Some Criticisms Considered

The faults frequently alleged against *The Man Who Loved Children* are overemphasis and excessive length; these criticisms appear in both the 1940 and the 1965 reviews. They are related charges and might be said to stem from the cause already noted in the discussion of *House of All Nations*, that is, Christina Stead's desire to submit her subject to a treatment which is both intense and thorough. Critics today seem less worried about overemphasis (leading to caricature) than they were in 1940. Perhaps the full implications of the new movements in twentieth-century fiction did not make themselves felt until the 1940's and 50's—Kafka, Faulkner, and Lawrence all had to wait till after World War II for proper recognition. There has been a boom in the allegorical—symbolic novel (of both past and present) in the last two decades and this has made readers less prone to dismiss a character as "exaggerated" if it seemed that the canons of realism were in any way flouted.

If World War II taught us anything it was that stranger and far less "credible" creatures than Sam were abroad—and plenty of them. Sam's speech is often inflated or bookish to an unnatural degree, but that is because he cannot help behaving like a cheap politician or a crank even within his own family—his personality always needs an audience. In literature very subtle lines distinguish the absurd human being from the grotesques like Quilp with only one leg in the real world, or these latter from monsters that have no human features at all. However much individual passages might offend our sense of what is plausible it is a mistake to fasten on them separately instead of trying to see them as part of that elaborate pattern which is a character entity. A really good novelist can get away with anything once his convictions become ours, that is, once he has established his hold over us. As far as Sam's ways of talking are concerned this takes Christina Stead no more than the first chapter and one of Sam's Sunday-Fundays. Thereafter we take this sort of thing in our stride, monstrous as it might appear in isolation, because essentially it is true to the nature of this man.

My Benjamin will be called Franklin, and I should put in Phoebus Apollo if I wanted to imitate those silly old Dagos what thought our beloved old Sol was a young man, a good-looker too; he was born at morning-rise, and I have just been giving him a serenade outside his window, not that he hears it yet. Morning is sacred; all great ideas are born in the morning or at midnight's starry clang. (p. 299)

"Impossible" when used to describe a person in real life means that he is behaving in an extreme, an unacceptable way. The novelist's job is to turn the real-life "impossible" into an artistic "possible" (or "probable," but the "possible" is sufficient). The best literature has never shrunk from extremes.

The charge of excessive length needs to be considered more closely. As so often, in matters of literary evaluation, we can go confidently part of the way so long as we insist upon the evidence, but we come finally into the realm of interpretation and opinion. Many critics have felt that *The Man Who Loved Children* is too long—among them some who still insist that the book is a masterpiece. Randall Jarrell believes that some of the material is either excessively detailed or redundant, and specifies Sam's welcome home party, Henny's tirades, Sam's orations, and the scenes at Harper's Ferry, Monocacy, and Annapolis. These, indeed (excepting Annapolis), are the parts that appear most open to criticism, but the allegation must be, I believe, an overabundance (of basic material) not irrelevance. This is obvious enough with Henny's tirades and Sam's speechifying; they are central to the characterization, but the point is how long the novelist should go on with

them. It could be argued, for example, that the last big row between Sam and Henny in the nightmarish final chapter, though
supposedly the worst ever, does not strike the reader that way; the
previous ones seem just as violent and, even, more memorable;
which is to say that coming earlier their impact is greater. Violence dulls with repetition. Christina Stead's main problem with
Henny is to sustain the hysterical element (which, though increasing as time passes, is strong from the start) without allowing it to
become excessive and tedious. She is largely successful, if only
because a novel offers more opportunities for relaxation of tension
than a play. We can see Henny happy (more or less) and at
leisure on occasions in different places, among different people.
Consequently though we see and hear much more of her than of
say, Maggie, in Tennessee Williams' *Cat on a Hot Tin Roof*, she is
less wearing on the nerves.

It is only fair to show more precisely the degree of relevance of
the other questionable parts. The Pollits' welcome-home party for
Sam has a more important function in the novel than Jarrell, by
implication, allows. It is the only occasion where Sam is in some
doubt about himself and his future. He has returned strangely
affected by the East, more thoughtful, more restrained toward his
children—in short, more like an adult. He has quarreled with
Colonel Willets, leader of the expedition, he is gloomy because the
children, forgetting him and their promises, have neglected the
house and grounds, and he seems for a time even out of sympathy
with the rest of the Pollits. On top of all this Henny deliberately
provokes him by drinking punch and then abuses him in front of
their own household and the Pollit clan. This scene (which runs to
sixteen pages) dramatizes the differences between the extroverted
Pollits with their irritating vitality on the one hand and the alien-
ated Henny and Louisa, inward-looking and self-absorbed, on the
other. And Sam for once feels lost, not that he ever identifies himself with his benighted and unprincipled relatives.

The finer shades apart, the whole scene is rendered with such
vivacity and such controlled dramatic effect that it should not be
considered overlong. The immediate consequence is the birth of
another child, which does not, of course, improve relations between
husband and wife, though Sam had hoped it would, but confirms
him in his old ways. The other big event that occurs at this time is
the death of David Collyer; this marks the turning point in Sam's

career. There follow the attacks on his reputation, the loss of his job, his further retreat from the adult world and the move to Spa House, which is the beginning of the end for Henny.

The other material in question is that which occupies the first three sections of Chapter 5. The first of these deals with the Bakens, Louisa's mother's people, at Harper's Ferry and Louisa's summer vacation visits—eleven pages in all and perhaps more than strictly necessary to establish the different stock from which Rachel came (old-fashioned religious) and the attraction the place has for Louisa. Sections 2 and 3 are set at Monocacy, Henny's family home. They have so much to contribute to the book's total meaning and make their points with such insight and humor that it would be churlish to find fault with them. Sam is overseas and Henny, though pregnant, is relaxed and in the mood for female gossip (at the same time doing her best to squeeze more money out of the family).

To Louisa this is very different from the idyllic world of Harper's Ferry; her idealizing tendencies give way to the fascination an incipient writer would feel for the raffish, somewhat decayed atmosphere that surrounds the Collyers—the old father and his mistresses, Barry the drunkard son, the smutty-minded servant girl, and going on all the time the talk, talk, talk of the women, macabre, scandalous, salacious, a revelation of the adult world. Henny's mother, the bawdy-tongued old Ellen is a superb character in miniature but no mere indulgence on the author's part. She confirms, but humorously, Henny's conviction that women always get a bad deal from life; Ellen has learned to accept. Admitting the worst gives you courage to face life and accustom yourself to its filth. Dirt is the recurring image of this scene—the dirt of marriage and families, fornication and cancer, drunkenness and brothels.

Henny laughed with irritation, "Let her stay, let her hear the dirt."
Old Ellen laughed, "You want to hear the dirt?"
"She's got her ears stuffed with dirt," said Henny. They all laughed good-naturedly. Old Ellen affected to disregard the child's blush and cried, "Well, I've got a head full of dirt. You could comb it out. These windy days I don't wash it for a sixmonth. Life's dirty, isn't it, Louie, eh? Don't you worry what they say to you, we're all dirty." (p. 181)

Old Ellen serves to throw Henny into sharper relief. She does not expect justice; she has produced her brood and her man can torment her no longer. She is made of sterner stuff than Henny, who finds her rather repulsive. Henny will not learn the ancient wisdom and so will not survive. When we add to this the talk about poisons and suicides, and the maid calling Louisa a bastard because she is "a norphan," we have assembled the evidence that enables us to say that the whole scene is carefully designed by way of allusion, parallel, contrast, and anticipation to fit into the general structure of the novel.

VII *Its Universality*

One other objection to *The Man Who Loved Children* should be mentioned—that it does not accurately depict American life of the time and place in which it is set. (It is risky for an Australian reader to try to adjudicate here, especially since for every American reviewer who takes this view another one, at least, can be found who says the opposite.) The reason that the fault-finders give is that *The Man Who Loved Children* is essentially an autobiographical novel (presumably Christina Stead's equivalent of O'Neill's *Long Day's Journey Into Night*) and that the novelist has simply transferred the Australian material to the American scene. To which it must be said that the value of this book as literature does not depend on its autobiographical element or its social reportage.

A study of family life as truthful as this must originate in personal experience, but the real novelist is never the slave of fact, even in a straight autobiographical novel, and anyone can see that there is more to *The Man Who Loved Children* than autobiography. It is a book which submits experience to imaginative reconstruction in its search for universal statements. Its universality, created like all genuine fiction through thousands of specific details, makes the Australian-American argument unimportant. As Eleanor Perry has so pungently said of the book's early critics who claimed that Christina Stead did not seem to catch the true flavor of an American family, "Perhaps they have ended up writing family situation comedies for television." [8] By the same token two occurrences of the word "corroboree," one reference to kangaroo (in a rhyme), one to an Australian possum, and the drinking of tea do not make an Australian book of it either. The essence of the book is the family as microcosm; its truth and power are everywhere apparent—from its largest gestures down to the revealing turn of a phrase: " 'I like your Clare,' said Sam. Louie perseveringly skinned her shoe on the curb" (p. 351). What it takes for granted are insights another novelist might be proud of; the children play on as the parents tear each other to pieces in the next room.

Jarrell is right when he claims that *The Man Who Loved Children* shows as few books have ever done, what family life is really like and right again to mention Tolstoy in the same paragraph. Reading this book takes the mind back to *The Kreutzer Sonata* and to *Anna Karenina*. *The Man Who Loved Children* is a novel that takes its own place in the great tradition of European fiction. It is too, and there is no contradiction here, a truly original work of art.

VIII   *Louisa and Teresa*

For Love Alone, as already pointed out, is related in theme and character to *The Beauties and Furies;* it also has its links with *The Man Who Loved Children*. Louisa asserts her independence before she reaches the age of fifteen by starting on her "walk around the world" as the book ends. Teresa in *For Love Alone* also has to throw off the family bonds (as well as other impediments) though she is a woman in her twenties before she does so and even then only half her story has been told. There are other similarities, allowing for their difference in age, between Louisa and Teresa. Both are avid readers, inspired by literature to seek new worlds in which to fulfill their imaginings and desires. Louisa's knowledge of a reality stronger than fairy tales comes through books that Sam gives her to correct her "unscientific mind"—unintentionally he reveals to her "the unspeakable madness of sensuality in past ages and concealed imaginations" (p. 379). Teresa peoples her solitude with her favorite private movies, more real than dull, ordinary life, and with fables of lust that come to her in the heat of the day.

There is a similarity too about the fathers. Andrew Hawkins has the same coloring and complexion as Sam; as the book opens he is standing naked, except for a towel rolled into a loincloth, in front of his two daughters, boasting about his idealism and his way with women, and orating in Pollit fashion on the virtues and beauties of love. But Andrew is to play a much less important part than Sam and after Chapter 1 he is little more than a presence behind the family scenes, which occur in the first half of the book only. *For Love Alone* ends up dramatizing a triangular relationship but, unlike *The Man Who Loved Children,* one character now occupies the center of the stage throughout. If Sam is the man who loved children, Teresa is the woman who loved love, and our reading of *For Love Alone* falls short of the book's demands if we fail to catch the ironical implications that Christina Stead brings to the story of a heroine for whom she has an obvious affection.

Both these novels deal with love—Sam's possessive, self-regarding, and destructive; Teresa's (despite its intensity) unselfish and, ultimately, liberating and creative. Jonathan Crow, who at first glance might seem to parallel Sam, turns out differently; he has his furtive affairs with servant women but is capable only of lust, not love. There is a cold perversity about Crow that makes him less attractive than Sam who, when all is said against him, gets some enjoyment from living. Sam at least believes in love; Crow's only enjoyment derives from denying or degrading it. To Teresa love is all; her book is the story of a search and for this reason *For Love Alone* also anticipates *Letty Fox,* which is a search for love by a different sort of woman in a different society.

In an article aptly entitled "The Bashful Bloke" Geoffrey Dutton comments on the extraordinary scarcity in Australian literature of poems and stories on the subject of love: ". . . in most of our prose and verse the only honoured image of love in the outback is that of the lonely wife on the far station, or the drover's wife left behind, a figure that haunted Henry Lawson." [9] And he goes on to say that if it were not for a few women writers love would emerge in Australian literature, with occasional exceptions, as a subject fit only for comedy. Dutton's "few women writers" would include Henry Handel Richardson and Christina Stead, and the obvious novels to choose would be *Maurice Guest* and *For Love Alone.*

IX   *Teresa's Search for Love*

The widower Andrew Hawkins lives with his two daughters Kitty and Teresa and his two sons Lance and Leo at the Bay by

the entrance to Sydney Harbour. The children have no respect or
affection for the father and, though fond enough of one another,
quarrel a good deal among themselves. Love (or the absence of
it) seems to dominate their lives. Lance, aged twenty-two, is overworked, lonely, and sex-starved. Kitty, the elder sister and household drudge, seems headed for spinsterdom. The engaging Leo,
aged seventeen, spends his spare time pursuing girls. Teresa, a
young schoolteacher who hates her job, dreams continually of
love, which she sees as her only means of escape from her frustrated life. Teresa, in fact, is obsessed with the idea of love. All the
young women she knows have the one ambition—to make a safe
marriage. Teresa wants marriage also but the kind she seeks is
different. She reads the erotic classics—they, she believes, are the
real thing, and she spurns the simpering obscenities of suburbia.
Her greatest fear is the spinsterdom which seems Kitty's fate,
something Kitty (to Teresa's delight) succeeds in avoiding. Teresa's determination to have love at any cost and her attraction
toward the intellectual life lead her to imagine she has found her
man in Jonathan Crow, a young graduate who coaches her in
Latin. Poverty also serves to strengthen the bond between them.
Through Crow she is given a taste of university life and when he
goes abroad to study, Teresa, though their relationship has obviously not yet developed into mutual love, resolves to remain faithful to him and join him in England as soon as she can. Teresa
idealizes the absent Jonathan and writes long letters to which he
occasionally replies, only to prevaricate or to retract some offer he
has previously made. Having given up teaching she gets a factory
job and practices the most rigorous economies to save up her passage money. She walks great distances to avoid tram fares and
eats so little that she becomes thin and ill.

If she won Jonathan Crow, it would be by superior will and intelligence; but this will and intelligence she had to devote to diverting
her passions, because she had evolved the curious idea that she
would only win Jonathan Crow by bridling passions as far as she
was able, because of Jonathan's own self-denial. (p. 256)

Teresa was almost twenty when Jonathan sailed for England; four
years of struggle and self-denial are to pass before she is able to
follow him. Crashaw's hymn to that earlier Teresa yields a couplet
appropriate to this stage in the novel:

> Since 'tis not to be had at home
> She'll travel to a martyrdom.

So ends "The Island Continent."

The second part, "Port of Registry: London," takes up the story of Teresa's life in England, where she arrives in May, 1936. Jonathan, whom Teresa knew as a thin-faced, struggling young intellectual, has become a self-assured man of the world. They are frequently in each other's company now and their relationship is accorded that close psychological scrutiny that marks *The Man Who Loved Children*. It becomes increasingly clear that Jonathan is incapable of any genuine affection and, consequently, unable to understand Teresa's belief in love or appreciate the sacrifices she has made for him. He simply uses his relation with her to satisfy his morbid fondness for self-analysis and what he likes to believe is a genuine scientific curiosity about human behavior. Despite her bewilderment and dismay at his cold and taunting treatment Teresa remains (or so she obstinately thinks) in love with Jonathan for some time yet.

Teresa's gradual awakening to the truth is hastened and completed by James Quick (her boss), an American businessman who falls in love with her and treats her as a woman and as an equal. She responds to Quick's love but will not yield to him until his wife (from whom he is separated) knows the truth. Once honor is satisfied she is prepared to take up connubial life with him. In the meantime Quick has put Jonathan in his place by exposing his intellectual pretensions, his academic mediocrity, and the shabbiness of his dealings with women. Having achieved love at last, Teresa now begins to rejoice in her newly found freedom and happiness and to want power over men. She develops a passion for Harry Girton, a radical who is about to join the International Brigade, spends a couple of days with him, and then returns to the devoted, unselfish Quick. She is tempted to go to Spain with Girton, but her loyalty to Quick prevails and she promises never to see Girton again: "'I don't think chastity and monogamy and all that is necessary, but somehow—I don't want you to think I love you less'" (p. 500). This declaration precedes the final scene in which Teresa glimpses Crow, like a villain in melodrama, skulking around the London streets at dusk. She laughs at the strange figure, he gives no sign of recognition. So little did she know of him that she can scarcely believe Quick when he tells her Crow is color blind.

For Love Alone matches The Man Who Loved Children in the power of its emotional conviction; such is Christina Stead's concentration here on the central character that the book develops an intensity of a more personal kind. Yet For Love Alone has implications extending beyond its account of individual experience—it also attempts to convey that peculiarly Australian feeling, a sense of isolation from the fountains of European civilization. It is, by a kind of reversal process, a book rich in cultural allusion and association. In the first place, it is built on the pattern of the physical and spiritual journey, hence the Ulysses references. The prelude "Sea People" emphasizes the Australian loneliness and ends thus:

It is a fruitful island of the sea-world, a great Ithaca, there parched and stony and here trodden by flocks and curly-headed bulls and heavy with thick-set grain. To this race can be put the famous question: "Oh, Australian, have you just come from the harbour? Is your ship in the roadstead? Men of what nation put you down—for I am sure you did not get here on foot?" (p. 2)

This passage is echoed by Teresa herself later on when she says to Jonathan:

"I was going to wonder if we wouldn't be different from all other races but the Egyptians perhaps, because of the sun, the desert, the sea—but our sea is different—each Australian is a Ulysses—'Where did you come from, O stranger, from what ship in the harbour, for I am sure you did not get here on foot?' " (p. 222).[10]

In the next chapter we read:

It was an accident, perhaps some early song, some tale of Britain, that made her think she could escape by sea. It was perhaps the first visions printed on her mind as a child of the sailors who, from de Quiros to Cook, had sailed all the seas and discovered Australia, and England's sea history, and the voice of the sea behind the language. She loved the sea with a first and last love, had no fear of it, would have liked to sail it for two years without seeing land; she had the heart of a sailor. How could she be satisfied on the dull shore? (p. 224)

The prelude seen in retrospect now takes on a greater significance, not unlike that of Fisherman's Bay in *Seven Poor Men of Sydney;* set at the portals of the island continent it looks out and away to other worlds.

The isolation of the white race in a newly conquered, remote, and ancient land is the theme of Kol Blount's legend of Australia in his memorial recitation for Michael toward the end of *Seven Poor Men of Sydney.* But whereas Michael becomes a victim of youthful despair, Teresa has goals to strive for. Catherine Baguenault is torn between the desire for marriage and the desire for a career; she wants love and freedom but cannot achieve them. Teresa finds the happiness that eludes Catherine because she has the determination to escape. (The final chapters of *For Love Alone* suggest, moreover, that she will combine marriage with a career.) She leaves Australia primarily because she believes she will find love with Jonathan in England; this motive is to the fore throughout and so strong does it become that her other impulses are lost to the reader's view in the central chapters. The Teresa of the early chapters is a young woman whose imagination has been fired by the masterpieces of European literature; she has other interests too, artistic and intellectual, which turn her mind toward the Old World. But so absorbed does the novelist become in exploring Teresa's emotional entanglement with Jonathan that the embryonic writer does not emerge till Chapter 34, by which time the book is more than three quarters done. It is in this chapter that Quick discovers Teresa's notes for "The Seven Houses of Love," after fuming over the psychological jargon and the pompous aridities of Crow's latest essay, "Meliorism, or the Best of Possible Worlds."

Douglas Stewart in an appreciative essay, in which he compares *For Love Alone* with the fiction of Conrad and Lawrence, finds some inconsistency in Christina Stead's presentation of Teresa.

The passion of the book, its restless impetus, comes from Teresa. In some respects she is not wholly credible as a character. Her complete rejection of love—except in Jonathan's letters—in the central chapters when she is starving and saving for her trip to London, seems inconsistent with the portrait drawn in the opening at Watson's Bay. Possibly this could be justified, outside the novel, by the explanation that the central chapters are skimped; but the objection would remain that here, as throughout the story (as indeed is admitted), Teresa is driven not so much by love as by "a great destiny." The novelist hints that Teresa will become a writer, but she has not stressed the point sufficiently. A fully convincing Teresa would have to be genius first and woman second; this one is the reverse.[11]

This amounts to saying that the real theme is not love but the emergence of the writer and that, artistically, the book is confused. But this, it seems to me, is to oversimplify the characterization and to deny the evidence. Teresa diverts rather than rejects love in Jonathan's absence and this is perfectly credible in such a strong and obsessive personality as hers. (We may recall her resistance, as a matter of principle, to Quick even after she has acknowledged her love for him.) And her sense of "a great destiny" (granting that it could have been given more emphasis) is not to be separated from her desire for the fulfillment of her whole nature. The artist in Teresa can find release only through the experience of love. Indeed, as the book ends there are potentialities for both her private life and a career, the extent of which we can only guess at. The whole book is, demonstrably, a study of a search for love; as it happens, Teresa is proved wrong, not about love, but in believing she was in love with Jonathan. When disillusionment begins to set in she can think of the past as "the rigmarole of her buffoon Odyssey" and, finally, she endorses Quick's assessment that " 'It was just the illusion of a love-hungry girl.' " Self-deception awaits the idealist, whether a Teresa or a Sam Pollit.

The theme finds expression in other sets of images too. One of these is drawn from that subject celebrated in French art, the journey to an island of blessedness, the voyage to Cythera. In conversation with Jonathan Teresa once refers to Watteau's "The Embarkation for Cythera," which symbolizes for her the mysteries of love and the access to all secret desires.[12] (Jonathan does not receive this confession at all sympathetically.) Yet another underpinning of the central theme occurs in a more complex way in the refashioning of certain imagery from Baudelaire, one of Christina Stead's favorite poets. But before going into details of this we should note how carefully (perhaps oversystematically?) the whole book is organized to reveal the different aspects and paradoxes of love and the stages the heroine passes through on her journey.

X *Structure and Imagery*

The Hawkins household (as already pointed out) is preoccupied with the idea of love in one form or another: the book opens with the father's prating about its beauty and wonder (it ends with Teresa's sighing for the suffering it causes); chapters 2 and 3 provide an unforgettably brilliant account of "the concupiscent fever" that rages, among young and old alike, at Malfi March's wedding. Teresa, longing for love and marriage, is both fascinated and repelled by the occasion—fascinated because it touches her deepest desires, repelled because it is enveloped in an atmosphere of sniggering, sexy excitement. After the wedding celebrations Kitty and Teresa go off with Aunt Bea, a wonderfully bawdy old character given to smutty talk, which shocks her daughter Anne. At the house where Aunt Bea rents rooms lives the neurotic woman who has rejected sex and whose husband is (consequently, according to Aunt Bea) in a lunatic asylum and daughter, boy-crazy.

At the end of Chapter 4 Teresa finds Anne in tears because she has not yet been able to marry. Chapter 5 describes the Bay at night as a "strange battlefield" of love. Chapters 6–8 explore Teresa's discontent, revealing her private fantasies and erotic thoughts, her desire for escape from this world of frustration. Sensing the same feeling in the others she continually urges Kitty and the brothers to marry and leave home. Before long she gives up her job and sets out on her long walk to Harper's Ferry— her first journey, but a bid for freedom that fails. In the country fresh images of love and lust haunt Teresa; "pale sterility" of Cousin Ellen at the age of twenty-nine, the necking party at the Carlin's house, the young man struck down by madness when about to be married and the girl still in love hopelessly waiting, the nightmarish scene with the old pervert on a lonely road. Even when Teresa joins Jonathan's discussion group at the University she finds herself among a group of female admirers who have created a kind of love-cult around their idol ("the gadfly of desire") and, as we might expect, love is a leading topic in the conversation and the letters that pass between Teresa and Jonathan. Teresa ultimately declares her love and the rest of "The Island Continent" concerns her devotion to him during the long years she must endure before she can join him in England.

The second half of the novel is as unremitting in its concentration on the same subject. It analyzes minutely the progress of what is now the decidedly curious relationship between Teresa and Crow. He is as much obsessed with sex as she ever was with love and marriage, but whereas her concern is open and honest, his is furtive, almost pornographic. Jonathan represents love twisted and soured. The chapters following Teresa's casting off of Jonathan are as clearly concerned with the same topic—now it is the different aspects love takes on in a woman free and conscious of her new powers. There can be no doubt that love is the real as well as the apparent theme; it is reinforced, moreover, in a poetic way that recalls the methods of the early books, though it must be added straightaway that the influence of Baudelaire, for example, is seen to different (and better) effect in *For Love Alone* than in *The Beauties and Furies.*

XI   *Name–Symbolism of the Main Characters*

Once more *Seven Poor Men of Sydney* is the seed-bed for later growth; the relevant passages come from one of Kol Blount's poetic orations on love, its possessiveness and powers of endurance: ". . . a strong passion moves in chaos and associates with death, its foot goes among hermits and ravens. Love, love passing through many frightful experiences, retchings and convulsions, draws sustenance from them; they only show it the measure of its fortitude. Even so its skin is dyed with the mess it feeds on, but it lives. From the fierceness of its discontent it craves all violences, pains and perversions, and feeds on its disappointments. . . . Venus should be black: that is the colour of love, the rite of the night" (pp. 61–62). These words prefigure part of Teresa's story —her love for Jonathan thrives, for years, on denial and disappointment, as if to prove Blount right when he concludes: "To love you must dissociate yourself from humanity, as with all great passions." *For Love Alone,* of course, moves beyond (or away from) Blount's romanticism to draw out the destructive and the creative potentialities of love. "Venus should be black," the foot of passion "goes among hermits and ravens"—a slide in emphasis and the object of Teresa's misguided passion becomes a dark, axe-faced young man named Crow. And it is into this complex of images that Baudelaire enters reinforcing the symbols of color and the journey.

In "Un Voyage à Cythère" the poet travels to the island of Love, and instead of its legendary beauty finds there a gibbet where hideous birds of prey feast on the body of a man, and animals prowl beneath. The poet likens his sufferings to what is happening to the corpse on the gallows—his flesh is torn too, in expiation for his sins committed in the cult of love, which deny him the protection of a tomb.

> "Devant toi, pauvre diable au souvenir si cher,
> J'ai senti tous les becs et toutes les mâchoires
> Des corbeaux lancinants et des panthères noires
> Qui jadis aimaient tant à triturer ma chair."

Teresa, likewise, makes her voyage in search of love, only to find disenchantment and pain—the bird of prey who feeds on her sufferings is Jonathan Crow.

Crow is one of the finest of Christina Stead's character studies. He is a thoroughly nasty, but perfectly credible fellow whose true nature is gradually revealed till he stands clear, first to us, then to Teresa, in his proper colors. If, as some critics have alleged, Crow is a monster, he is so only in the sense that Sam Pollit is—as a figure drawn with such intense conviction and concentrated power that he becomes truly memorable. This is a penetrating and merciless study of a superficially bright young scholar in love with his own brilliance, which consists largely in mouthing all the currently "advanced" platitudes about free thought and free love to his bevy of (mainly female) admirers.

Born into a poor family (and he never really outgrows the bitterness poverty has bred in him) Crow has risen to modest eminence in university life and bathes in the admiration of those earnest, pathetic souls who inhabit its cultural fringe. He has some reason to be proud of his achievement and if only for this has claims on the reader's sympathy; however, he works out his grudges against society not only by his rather adolescent social theorizing but also by exploiting the women who admire him. Jonathan is continually dramatizing the one subject—himself; full of self-pity, insecurity and conceit he prevaricates and rationalizes to satisfy his need to dominate and his desire for self-aggrandisement. He shamelessly exploits Teresa's genuine, almost desperate love for him, toying with her affection, leading her on and then

rebuffing her—all this after the self-denial and poverty she has
endured in order to join him.

Intellectually and emotionally perverted, he is pleased to describe himself as a social scientist studying in Teresa an example
of masochism and mythomania. " 'She wants me but I've got her
trimmed, it's an interesting little case in psychology, by Jove!' "
(p. 385). His endless theorizings about love (all mixed up with his
own personal problems), on sadism and masochism, on homosexual love as more logical than heterosexual, love as paranoia and so
on are, like his pretentious formalizations of social and moral issues, but a cover for his vanity and hollowness. James Quick, who
has a nice turn of phrase, once sums him up: " 'The stifled bestial-
ity of the monastery, the crackpot egotism of the cracker-barrel
sage'" (p. 416). Just as Crow means to Teresa denial and frustration or death, so Quick, as his name suggests, means life; she says
to James, " '. . . you've restored me to life. . . . I was dead to
the world'" (p. 367). Quick is as sensitive to her sufferings as
Crow is indifferent (that is, when he is not positively rejoicing in
them).

Christina Stead's heroine is a twentieth-century Saint Teresa, in
her own way, seeking fulfillment in the union of human, as Saint
Teresa sought it in divine, love. One might take some of St. Teresa's own words to express this longing. "This soul longs to be
free. Eating is killing it, sleep brings it anguish. It sees itself wast-
ing the hours of this life in comforts, though nothing can comfort
it now but You. It seems to be living unnaturally, since now its
desire is to love not in itself but in You." [13] This parallelism is
worked out in more specific ways too. In her mystical treatise, *The
Interior Castle,* which originated in one of her visions, Saint Teresa
describes the Seven Mansions of the Soul. In the powerful, nightmarish scene in the deserted sawmill where Teresa and Jonathan
spend some of their last hours together, Teresa thinks " 'This is the
last of the Houses of Love,'" and then, suddenly, as if struck by a
vision, " 'How stupid he is! How dull!' " (p. 408). This is the end
of their relationship. It is in the following chapter that Quick calls
on Teresa and sees her notes for the book she is trying to write
called "The Seven Houses of Love," a book about the sorrows of
women. The astonished Quick, who is just beginning to realise
how much Teresa has suffered has, only half an hour before, been
reading Crow's perverse and pretentious essay on "Meliorism," in

which he has come across this passage about womankind, saints
and libertines alike:

> Women are brought up to the hunt, men left the hunt long ago,
> women cannot be modern till they cease to hunt men, . . . we can
> do without the St. Teresas as well as the legendary libertine, coiling
> herself like a serpent in the poisonous dew of men's lasciviousness
> which without her would not exist, sterile Paphian, superfoetation of
> Pauline sexual fears. (p. 417)

Not only does this draw attention once more to the heroine's nature but it also echoes the imagery of the hunt that is used by
Teresa herself in one of the most important of her early self-
communings.

> A woman is a hunter without a forest. There is a short open season
> and a long closed season, then she must have a gun-licence, signed
> and sealed by the state. There are game laws, she is a poacher, and
> in the closed season she must poach to live. (p. 75)

In these two passages the same basic idea occurs but the connota-
tions are worlds apart. It needs a Quick to endorse the truth of
what a woman feels and allow her to be different from men. Crow
is shrewd enough to know, in Quick's words, that woman is
haunted by the fear of biological failure, and heartless enough to
exploit that weakness.

Christina Stead's fiction has sometimes been said to sacrifice
form for life. Among the later books *Letty Fox* is a test case, but
For Love Alone is certainly a well-constructed novel. The elabora-
tion of its details for purposes of counterpoint and comment (as
in this instance of the hunting imagery) is another feature of its
firmly woven pattern. Indeed the dissatisfaction many readers feel
with Quick may derive from an overplaying of contrasts in the interest of theme. The structure needs a counterbalance to Crow
and his effect upon the heroine, and this is what Quick provides,
but, despite his name and his energetic nature, he is never as convincing a character as Crow. He is Teresa's knight-errant and his
assigned role dominates him as an individual. Potentially a richer
and more attractive personality he never becomes as interesting as
his distasteful rival. This, no doubt, is partly because he is less

closely studied, but here, as so often in literature, the villain steals
the show from the hero. Even after Crow has been vanquished
Quick takes a decidedly second place to the newly emerging heroine.

She was too formed by adversity and too firm and ambitious by nature to take pleasure in her marital union alone. It was scarcely Quick
who had done it, but fate. . . . (p. 458)

XII   *An Unromantic Ending*

The final insights of the novel are, rightly, Teresa's. As a
woman she sees differently from Quick and beyond his range, despite his superior knowledge and intellect. When Teresa tries to
tell the whole truth about her feelings James is upset because hers
is not the romantic love he expected. She realizes her mistake and
exerts herself to charm him back again. But she knows that from
now on "each day would be a step farther into the labyrinth of
concealment and loving mendacity." And she goes on to reflect:

"I belong to the race which is not allowed to reason. *Love is blind*
is the dictum, whereas, with me at least, Love sees everything. Like
insanity, it sees everything; like insanity, it must not reveal its
thoughts." (p. 460)

The woman and the artist are beginning to flower in Teresa, and
Quick realizes that the life he has been offering her will not satisfy an individual "idea-hungry, ambitious and energetic."

It is the unconventional ending of Teresa's story (especially her
passionate interchange with Harry Girton) that has worried some
critics, who seem to feel that Teresa now loses all her dignity. But
Christina Stead's concern is with the truth, not to fob the reader
off with a romantic, happy-ever-after ending. Teresa's restlessness,
her sense of awakened powers, emotional and intellectual, and
her desire for freedom are much more in keeping with the rebellious, idealizing young woman of the early chapters than a passive
and contented wife would be. One reply to Douglas Stewart's criticism that Teresa should have been a genius first and a woman
second is that *For Love Alone* traces the steps by which the
woman comes to the threshold of maturity, a point at which her
genius has the chance to develop. The ending of *For Love Alone*

is artistically satisfying; furthermore, the final stages of the book justify the claim that Teresa is one of Christina Stead's most interesting and most complex character studies.

In *Middlemarch* George Eliot writes of the modern Teresas whose "ardour alternated between a vague ideal and the common yearning of womanhood; so that the one was disapproved as extravagance and the other condemned as a lapse." Her heroine, Dorothea Brooke, suffers the fate of many ardent young women whose aspirations (unlike those of the Spanish saint) are doomed to failure. The last sentence of the "Prelude" anticipates Dorothea's end: "Here and there is born a Saint Theresa, foundress of nothing, whose loving heart-beats and sobs after an unattained goodness tremble off and are dispersed among hindrances, instead of centering in some long-recognisable deed." [14]

Teresa Hawkins is made of sterner stuff. The epigraph to her story comes from the Prologue to *Don Quixote,* a part of the dialogue in sonnet form between Babieca (the Cid's famous steed) and Rocinante (the Don's hack). Rocinante complains of being starved and overworked, and when Babieca charges him with talking like an ass, he says (of his master),

> A lifelong ass is he—at least not clever—
> And in love the biggest ass was ever seen.

The following two lines, the second of which is the epigraph to *For Love Alone,* are:

B.   To love is foolish then?   R.   It is not wise.
B.   You grow metaphysical.   R.   From lack of food.[15]

A sardonic allusion to Teresa's mistakes and sufferings in the name of love, which, once again, underlines the detachment Christina Stead preserves, even when the entire novel is, basically, a rendering of intensely personal experiences from the viewpoint of the heroine.

For Love Alone first appeared during the war years and has not since been reissued in the United States; consequently it is less well known there than it deserves to be. It is still in a position similar to that of *The Man Who Loved Children* before its republication in 1965. It does not match *The Man Who Loved Children* in dramatic strength and characterization, but it is a book comparable in stature. If only because of the setting (and its thematic implications) it is likely to remain a favorite among Australian readers. It contains, among other things, some of the finest scenes Christina Stead has ever written—two of these call for special mention. The first is Chapter 3, "Malfi's Wedding," which creates the rowdy, bawdy gaiety of the occasion with an irresistible vitality and which, at the same time, manages to convey the yearnings and frustrations that lie beneath.[16] The second, in an entirely different vein, is the scene in the deserted sawmill (Chapter 33) which, in effect, marks the end of the strange, tormented relationship between Teresa and Jonathan. The decaying building, in which they take shelter from a storm that has caught them on a country walk, has an atmosphere of weirdness and horror which gradually generates fear in them both and hostility to one another. This is the last of Teresa's Houses of Love, "the last Star or Extinction" envisaged in her notes for "A System by which the Chaste can Know Love"; as the old mill wheel starts to turn and threatens to tear the building apart, Jonathan, suddenly deciding he can catch the 11 P.M. train back to London, abandons her there for the night.

CHAPTER 5

American Scenes

I The Alleged Failure of the Later Books

RANDALL Jarrell is wrong when he says baldly that *The Man Who Loved Children* was a complete failure on its first appearance. In fact it drew a number of appreciative reviews from responsible critics in America[1] (it has had its admirers in Australia for the last twenty years) and there is every reason to believe it would have continued to sell but for certain difficulties (not only associated with the European war) that stood in the way of further printings. So, even though the book did not win the recognition it deserved until 1965, it is misleading of Jarrell to describe it as a rejected masterpiece, and even wider of the mark to suggest that its unfavorable reception had a crippling effect on Christina Stead's subsequent work. Assuming that greater concentration on a central character does not necessarily mean limitation in vision and power we might ask, in what respects is *For Love Alone* a more "limited" book than *The Man Who Loved Children?* Whatever might be urged against it, *For Love Alone* is certainly not the work of a timid or a disappointed writer. No one would argue that the books which follow reach the level of these two, but it is unfair to discount them altogether as Jarrell seems to do. Furthermore, *Letty Fox* suffers for reasons other than those that Jarrell's "limitations" charge suggests; there is some failure in artistry here, but *Letty Fox* is a book full of life and rich in satiric observation, and a fairer estimate is possible by comparing it with the panoramic *House of All Nations* rather than with *The Man Who Loved Children*. The attractive *The People with the Dogs* (admittedly a work on a smaller imaginative scale than *The Man Who Loved Children*) reveals the writer striking out in new directions.

II *Popular Fiction?*

Another general criticism that has been leveled against the later
novels is that they are designed for the popular market. Cecil
Hadgraft says that *The Man Who Loved Children, Letty Fox,*
and *A Little Tea, a Little Chat* all tend in one direction, "the
providing of reading matter demanded by a large public." What
The Man Who Loved Children is doing in that list is anyone's
guess and no guess could possibly justify its inclusion, but, this
apart, the charge of writing down to put sales up (and it must
mean this) is the last criticism, whether one likes her work or not,
that could fairly be applied to Christina Stead, as any person who
has bothered to acquaint himself just with the details of her career
would know. Similarly, Miles Franklin, after inveighing against
Seven Poor Men of Sydney, writes: "Christina Stead has since
been lost to Australian novels, though the first part of *For Love
Alone* is set in Sydney. Abroad she has written fiction as impressive as any of the top shelf, and more recently stories almost as
bright as the romances of Marcia Davenport or other best-sellers.
Will she, one day, like Henry Handel Richardson return to her
birth soil to reach full stature?" [2] Why Miles Franklin should lament the loss when she found *Seven Poor Men of Sydney* a nasty
and pretentious book it is hard to say. It is apparent from the last
sentence of the quotation that Christina Stead's only hope of re-
demption is to return to Australia and Australian subjects. Hadgraft seems to think likewise, for he concludes: "It seems unlikely
that she will ever give us another Australian novel." [3]

The reader in search of popular spicy or romantic fiction would
soon be put off by the sheer volume of diverse material that *Letty
Fox* contains. It is a long, closely documented novel, packed with
characters, which sets Letty's struggles for emancipation and fulfilment against the background of her parents' broken marriage,
the matrimonial tangles of her relatives, against the hectic politics
of the 1930's, and the war and the post-war years in New York.
The tempestuous Letty hurls herself into the thick of things,
whatever she is doing—into childhood games with her sister Jacky
(Jacqueline), into all the activities at college, into her jobs in the
commercial world, into life at Greenwich Village, into leftist politics and into literature, and, of course, into her many love affairs.
But if the "popular" reader ever gets as far as these he will be

disappointed because they are not treated romantically nor are they described with the detail that many self-consciously out-spoken novelists of our day insist on in the name of truth. Letty tells her own story and the first chapter makes it clear that there will be nothing here for the smut-hunter.

Men don't like to think that we are just as they are. But we are much as they are; and therefore I have omitted the more wretched details of that close connection, that profound, wordless struggle that must go on in the relation between the sexes. I have come to the conclusion that it must go on and that certain realities of love between men and women should not be told.[4]

III   Letty Fox: *The Plan and The Story*

In an article published in the *Sydney Daily Telegraph* of Octo-ber 25, 1947, Christina Stead is reported as saying that she de-cided to write *Letty Fox* as a result of stupid American critical reaction to *For Love Alone.*

In that novel I tried to present a girl of no social background who just believed in love, but whom society forced into the same sordid mess that entrapped Letty Fox. American critics couldn't understand this girl, so I decided to give them someone they could understand— a young, pretty New York girl, talented, with a good social back-ground, who nevertheless finds promiscuity necessary in her search for security.

Letty Fox is divided into two parts. Book One, entitled "With the Others," fills in the family background and traces Letty's life up to the age of fourteen. Book Two, "On My Own," goes through the experiences of adolescence, Letty's jobs, her political activi-ties, her hobbies, her love affairs, her desperate attempts to find a husband and her success finally, in 1945, when she nails one of her old friends, Bill Van Week. This novel is built partly on the paral-lel, growing into a contrast, between Letty and her sister Jacky (one year younger). The two girls grow up in a divided family—a third girl, Andrea, is some years younger. Their father, Solander, is a gay, intelligent, liberal-minded man, who becomes estranged from his weak-willed and querulous wife, Mathilde, and can never thereafter be lured away from his mistress Persia, who be-comes in effect his second wife. Letty and her father remain on good terms; she is far fonder of him than of her mother and, thus, early in life grows accustomed to the idea of collapsing families and extra-marital love—commonplaces in American society of the 1920's and 1930's. The antics of her relatives, particularly the money-hunting Grandmother Morgan and uncles Philip and Percival (both of whom are in jail at the same time on charges of back alimony), and the corrupt and self-indulgent society in which she grows up confirm Letty in her free and easy ways. Her early years pass between America, England, and France as Mathilde follows Solander around in half-hearted attempts to patch up the broken marriage. Letty, by nature a high-spirited, energetic girl, is far from unhappy (though the early experiences, as the reader is expected to observe, leave their scars) and at the age of fourteen feels on top of the world. "Mathilde always asked why she was ever born and why no luck had ever come her way. I felt in my rather strident way, that my life was my luck. I could make the best of it" (pp. 164–65). By this age Letty, as we might guess, has a keen appreciation of what money can do.

Book Two opens with Letty almost sixteen and eager for fresh experiences. Within a year she falls in love with an intellectual and aristocrat, an Englishman, Clays Manning, who promises to divorce his first wife and marry Letty. Both Letty and Clays, it need hardly be said, are enthusiastic leftists. Her affair with Clays gradually fades out; put to the physical test he proves impotent and after a time leaves America for Spain and the Civil War. Letty's first lover is a rather weedy college professor, Amos, for whom she imagines she has a great passion—in fact her affair with him is created by curiosity about sex, boredom, impatience, and disappointment with Clays. Amos (already married) gets rid of her as soon as he can, Letty has an abortion and, back in society again, joins Jacky's art class, conducted by the celebrated teacher, Lucy Headlong. Mrs. Headlong becomes overfond of her but by now Letty has developed a passion for Luke Adams, a middle-aged married man, a friend of her father's, who has a reputation as a womanizer. Luke, as she says at the time, is the only man she ever loved madly and the inevitable break with him is a bitter blow. She takes up with the rich and handsome Bill Van Week but, disillusioned when she learns that Clays has ended up marrying another woman, decides that her only hope lies in a safe marriage. Letty has a number of others before she finally marries Bill;

she is attracted more now to middle-aged married men, the security of whose lives she wishes to share—the psychoanalyst she visits tells her, of course, that all this expresses a desire to marry her father. A point to be considered by those critics who brand Letty simply as a fortune hunter is that though she marries the son of a millionaire she knows that his father, who has other plans for Bill, will almost certainly disinherit him—and this is exactly what happens. Nevertheless as she brings her story to an end Letty is happy in the present and hopeful for the future.

IV   *Is the Novel Formless?*

Letty Fox has been severely handled by many reviewers, including some who admire Christina Stead's previous work. Sometimes a moral disapproval of the heroine prevents a just evaluation of the book, so that the critic spends his space condemning Letty or insisting that she is not a typical American girl. A more common objection is that the book is formless.

In one of the best of the early notices Mary McGrory[5] argues that the book falls between the satirical and the picaresque, a view which overlooks the fact that the picaresque novel is traditionally a means toward satire as well as a form of straight narrative. It is true, however, that the picaresque element in *Letty Fox* does tend to obscure the shape of the narrative, and this leads to the allegation of formlessness. In fact, a pattern of progression *is* to be detected in Letty's search for love (to confine the discussion, for the moment, to this theme); and the method is similar to that employed in the first part of *For Love Alone*.

Book One of *Letty Fox* is designed to establish the character of the heroine and to account for it (partly) in terms of the early environment; thereafter Letty, like Teresa, but more directly involved than she, goes through various stages of love—the process is a kind of sentimental education; and if Letty has learned less at the end than Teresa this is simply to say that she is a different kind of woman. There is the idealism and romance of youth in her love for Clays; curiosity about sex with Amos; a desire for affection and respectability with the medical student Bobby Thompson.

What proves to be the turning point occurs in the central section of Book Two, which contrasts two kinds of love and their effect on the heroine. One is the homosexual, which threatens

Letty in her relationship with the lesbian Lucy Headlong, and the other, the heterosexual, which is consummated in the fullness of physical passion with Luke Adams. It is significant that Lucy should express her hatred of Adams, as she fears he will take Letty from her; he does so, because Letty's affair with him begins in earnest after her return from the first visit to Lucy's country home—she can only dispel the edginess and frustration she brings back to New York by reaching out for genuine sexual fulfilment. Society frustrates Letty now; Luke she can never have to herself so she casts around desperately, at first for forgetfulness in brief affairs with others, and then, with growing determination, for marriage and security, or failing that, just marriage, to save herself from the aimlessness of promiscuity. Other experiences, too, interfere in the later stages of her search—notably her association with Amy Bourne and Edwige, and finally, as the circle brings us back to the family again, the incident involving her young sister Andrea and Andrea's girl friend Anita, and the death of Uncle Philip.

Amy Bourne is the careerist pure and simple, without malice, but a professional coach in the ways of trapping men into marriage. Edwige (a larger scale version of the evil young girl Sylvia in "The Triskelion") is far worse; she is cold, selfish, and ruthless and will destroy anyone who stands in the way of her insatiable greed. Letty rejects both of these women and what they represent. The critics who complain of the heroine's immorality apparently fail to see that real evil resides in the inhuman Edwiges, not in the muddled, well-meaning, and rather pathetic Letty Foxes of the modern world. Letty's assessment of herself in Chapter 1 is basically true. "I was one of those marrying women who married even her casual lovers: I had a very honest instinct" (p. 8).

The strange, but credible affair of the youngster Anita and her illegitimate child confirms Letty's desire for marriage. She sees the woman emerging in the boy-mad Andrea and feels the dignity that motherhood confers even upon the silly, misguided girl. Letty, it must be insisted, does learn something; she realizes now, for instance, that certain ultimates cannot be denied but will reassert themselves in the face of the greatest changes.

The family went on in the same old way after this scandal and I began to see that was what the family and society were for—to scatter during bomb-shells and then calmly cultivate the back-yard. Even the individual lives much on that plan. Letty next door to a fancy-girl; Jacky gone off into the blue beyond after an old philosopher; Andrea doting on an illegitimate baby; and the Family plodded along as if nothing had happened. (p. 486)

At this point Letty loses her present man, Cornelis. Finally there is Uncle Philip, cowed at last by the domineering Dora, the man who has lived for love and never found it, a kind of soul-mate to Letty. He walks away from Grandmother Morgan's party and hangs himself. Letty says: "He died for love. But I don't want to" (p. 493).

A genuine novel creates its own form, and to say this is not to deny the possibility of classifying novels according to certain major types. It does mean that the critic should not confuse form with formula. It is pointless, for example, to take exception to *Letty Fox* (as some have done) because it reaches no recognizable climax or because we cannot be sure if Letty will be content in marriage now that she has at last achieved it. There is demonstrably an organization of material toward clearly defined ends; Letty's experiences are so arranged, as in the Luke-Lucy sequences, as to provide their own implicit commentary. This grows outward from the characterization of the heroine toward a view of the society in which she lives.

Letty's search for love becomes a journey through society and, in the picaresque manner, a medium for social criticism. R. G. Howarth is wrong when he says this novel "celebrates female freedom." [6] It is a search, not a celebration. Letty's promiscuity is not freedom; her desire for freedom tangles with her need for security and she comes gradually to stake all on marriage. Within this society nothing more promising offers itself. *Letty Fox* is, obviously, an exposure of American sexual attitudes and marriage customs and what redeems Letty herself is the fact that, with all her faults, she is a better person than those who trade in marriage and divorce. She is by nature impulsive, generous, and open-hearted, and she finds herself in a society which rewards instead the selfish, the aggressive, and the materialistic. Since the moral implications of the book are unimpeachable, any criticism made must be for artistic reasons.

V An Accumulation of Detail

Letty Fox is firm enough in its general structure. It does, however, suffer from an overelaboration of detail and this is what has led some to call it formless. Is all of the family history in Book One necessary? And granting the significance of the principal relationships Letty contracts in Book Two, is there not some material that could be dispensed with or drastically reduced? The interlude at Susannah Ford's comes to mind. Another instance comes from the chapters dealing with Grandmother Fox and her niece Lily. The desire for social documentation means that Letty has to be exposed to many kinds of situations, involved in numerous activities, and the effect of all this experience on her conveyed through the necessarily limited first person narrative that Christina Stead has chosen. This is the only one of her novels cast in the autobiographical form, and the wisdom of the choice is in doubt.

VI Narrative Method

The dissatisfaction many readers have felt with *Letty Fox* stems probably more from the kind of narrative that Christina Stead has adopted than from anything else. Despite the use of the first person, Letty is not created as richly as the previous heroine, Teresa. This may be caused by the author's being less deeply involved; it is certainly due partly to the fact that Letty's inner life is not central to the book as was Teresa's in *For Love Alone*. Characters cannot be explored as thoroughly by a novelist who has one eye on the social scene at the same time. Moreover Letty herself, who is given to action rather than reflection, is potentially a less complex person than Teresa, and, for all her political and literary interests, less intelligent too. Consequently, though she is by no means unsympathetically presented (Mary McGrory complains that the satire is applied to all except the heroine) she wins less support than she needs. Here too the narrative method seems to tell against the characterization; the pace in Book Two is hectic and Letty is put through so many scenes in quick succession that, as when watching an old movie, we never seem able to look at the character in repose long enough to establish the proper focus. Book Two, despite all its action, develops a certain monotony, owing to insufficient variation in the pace of the narrative and a predictability as to the outcome of most of the events. The two excellent scenes set in Lucy Headlong's country home owe some of their success to the variety they provide the reader; in their strangeness and stillness they invite him to pause and brood and in so doing they become memorable.

In its wealth of incident, its narrative pace, and its placing of the heroine at a point where many social forces may impinge on her, *Letty Fox* is rather like Joyce Cary's *A Fearful Joy*. And like *A Fearful Joy* it falls below the level of the author's best work.

VII   *Is the Heroine Typical?*

In *Letty Fox* the narrator is sometimes more a hindrance than a help. First there is the matter of the typicality of the heroine; Letty describes herself as "just a run-of-the-mill New York girl" (p. 9) and rounds off the first chapter as follows: "I have written everyday facts, which, doubtless, have happened in the life of almost every New York middle-class girl who has gone out from high school or college to make a living in the city" (p. 12). The tantalizing thing about first person narrative is that we can never be sure if what the narrator says is true, even if he himself thinks it is, or (putting it more precisely) if what the narrator says is what the author for the present purposes believes to be true. Letty's own estimate seems to be close to the author's, in the light of Christina Stead's short prefatory note: "The language and opinions are those of a type of middle-class New York office worker."

One complication that develops later concerns the reliability of the narrator. She is, clearly, not always to be trusted and the questions then arise: Can we, the readers, always be sure where we stand in relation to Letty? Is she being viewed ironically or not? Does the author's attitude toward her fluctuate? Some critics have objected that Letty is not a typical New York girl; some, morally upset, have yelled "Slander!" "Typical" is a question-begging term. Letty is certainly not typical in the sense of "numerically average," but there is no reason whatsoever to doubt Christina Stead's claim that Letty is an accurately described example of a certain type, and that there were plenty of girls like her in New York at the time in which the novel is set. Letty is typical in wanting to be at one with her particular group:

For a long time now I had been working with people with the same
underlying political philosophy, the same esthetic creed, the same
over-all interests in life, the same love-lives, almost; the same advanced, sophisticated views on things like psychoanalysis, divorce,
writing, new trends in the movies. (p. 448)

This could be what the author means in her prefatory note, but, if
so, there would seem to be nothing gained by making Letty describe herself as a run-of-the-mill New York girl. Is there some
inconsistency in the characterization of Letty? Is she not decidedly more than "average sensual woman"?

In some ways Letty is quite a prodigy as, indeed, she herself
realizes. At the ages of eight and nine Jacky and she are "sopping
up Dostoevsky" (p. 117); at fourteen she writes her father a long
and self-consciously brilliant letter that might have come from a
bright undergraduate; just turned twenty Letty is one of those
well-educated young Radicals who take the Razumovsky Quartets
and Boileau's "L'Art Poétique" in their stride, have a passion for
Proust and can quote him in the original. Jacky's letters at the age
of fourteen make her even more precocious than Letty.

VIII   *The Degree of Self-Deception*

It looks as if Letty is given more accomplishments and talents
than she needs or ought to have, as if the author has invaded the
character instead of allowing her to remain herself. Letty, the
young woman, sometimes appears to lack the intelligence and insight that other parts of the book (both early and late) attribute
to her. An example of her muddled thinking comes in Chapter
XLII, which relates her encounter with the psychoanalyst. She is
told by her present lover, Wicklow, that she lacks sex-appeal, and
is persuaded to consult a friend of his, a fashionable psychoanalyst. The tone of Letty's account of her visit to the eminent man is
irreverent and debunking; she is horrified at his fees ($40 a
week), doubts his ability, and yet is pleased with his appearance:
"It was an honour to be his patient and, indeed, I felt at once that
I could love him; and that perhaps, up till now, I had not met the
right type of man. My father had always told me I would be better off with professional men" (p. 467). She tells her father she
must have the treatment; he refuses to pay, and Persia recom-
mends her to go to a fortuneteller instead. This Letty does and

finds most amusing, but she is impressed by the prediction that she will have an affair with a man whose initials are T or B, because she knows a man with both these—Tom Bratt. So she visits Bratt (a married man) the same evening and straightaway is planning a rendezvous with him. This is most amusing—and bewildering. Could she be such a fool, or such a self-deceiver? She chops and changes so quickly in the course of five pages that her behavior becomes incredible—unless we assume that she is hoaxing the other characters, and this seems most unlikely. Letty sometimes reminds us of Moll Flanders, who appeals so much to Defoe's sense of delight that every now and then she takes control of the author and runs clean away from the purpose and design of his novel.

The self-deception in the scene just referred to is marked enough to suggest that Letty is being treated ironically. On other occasions the ironical implications are unmistakable because she gives herself away so completely:

I had left the publishing office some weeks back, for the usual reason. The head of the office had started fooling round with one of the other girls, and I couldn't stand this indignity. I seized the first honourable occasion, this time a question of falsifying news, to quit. (p. 469)

But once invited to distrust Letty's account (and she obviously rationalizes a good deal) the reader may not know where his skepticism should stop. There are, moreover, occasions when Letty seems aware that she is deceiving herself and is determined to go on doing so, as in her attitude toward Clays (p. 25). The reader's problem is further complicated by the fact that Letty suffers intensely and can write and speak so forcefully that her words often demand his acceptance and approval.[7] Letty is a puzzle and, as a narrator, a decided risk.

IX   *Point of View*

The first person narrative is under pressure again, in more limited ways, in the earlier parts of the book. Letty, now at the age of twenty-four, begins to tell of her childhood; certain descriptions (e.g., pp. 16–17) will pass, so long as we insist upon a wit and intelligence well above average. So too the reader can accept the detachment with which she describes her roughness as a child, but he may find the narrative convention in Chapter II strained when the child's repeating of scenes and discussions is given in adult terms (pp. 21–22). What follows offers no difficulty because narrative and descriptive comment from the viewpoint of the adult narrator precedes the dialogue and so the reader unconsciously accepts it. Here the convention does not obtrude, but from now on the reader is occasionally jolted back into awareness of it, as when Letty is put into positions for overhearing adult conversations.[8] Similarly when Solander tells his daughters (aged eight and nine) that he must take them to see Persia because, though he can lie to their mother, he cannot lie to little girls, the author is trying to cover up the real reason, which is that she must get Letty into Persia's household to show us what is going on there. Further fractures of the convention occur when the omniscient narrator suddenly takes over; the description of Mrs. Looper clearly comes, not from Letty but from the author herself.[9] Then there are occasions when we feel it is the author and not the character speaking, as in the vigorous diatribe given to Pauline on the state of American womanhood (p. 133).

The central criticisms offered here of *Letty Fox* are that the technique is not adequate to the demands placed upon it and that Letty, as a character, does not properly fit the role assigned to her. In the scope of its social observation *Letty Fox* is closer to *House of All Nations* than to any other of Christina Stead's novels and a comparison between them is revealing. *House of All Nations* is superior for several reasons, the following among them: its social comment, not depending on a single character within the novel, is more comprehensive and objective; its theme is clearer and more firmly developed; its main characters are intrinsically more interesting.

X   *The Comedy*

Letty Fox does not stay in the mind with the conviction of a total experience like *The Man Who Loved Children* and (whatever its youthful faults) *Seven Poor Men of Sydney*. It is overlong, an uneven book but very good in places. A number of its best scenes occur in Book One: the incisive pictures of childhood in the accounts of Letty and Jacky and the different forms their wild activities take; impractical, likeable, amorous Uncle Philip,

arriving at Mathilde's flat on the eve of her departure for England
to face four women, who all come on the promise of a trip abroad;
and most of the scenes involving Grandmother Morgan, another
of Christina Stead's gallery of wonderfully bawdy old women, who
advises her weak-kneed daughter how to handle her erring husband:

> "Wear him down. And the other thing."
> "He'll say I've trapped him."
> "You are supposed to. Why do you think laws were made? Otherwise
> all our fine feathered friends would be running out on us all the time.
> Your father, you know, Mattie, had some cutie or other the whole
> time as far as I know. I simply took no notice. Men invented the
> tourist business. We can't take notice of that. The only trouble with
> modern women is they take it to heart. Forget it. You marry a man.
> You expect him to keep on bringing you candy and flowers. Forget it.
> You can't get men to wear their home address on their—collar." (p.
> 106)

The comedy Grandmother Morgan provides is all the richer for
being unconscious: "'You must sacrifice yourself for Tootsy and
Jacky,' said Grandmother heroically. 'I swear to you, Mattie, I
never had anything serious to do with a man till all you children
were grown up. I had a sense of duty'" (p. 107). The novelist's
ear for speech is as keen as ever in this book; a good example is
the scene in Chapter XXIV where Letty, almost sixteen, is out to
shock timid Grandmother Fox with an exaggerated account of a
wild New Year's party.

XI *Poetic and Symbolic Touches*

The satirist does not drive the poet right out of the book. Of
Grandmother Fox and Lily Christina Stead writes: "These silences between them, in their hour-long conversations, were like
the silences between birds settling for the night" (p. 77). And on
a larger scale there are the two strangely haunting and haunted
scenes set at Arnhem, Lucy Headlong's country house. For parallels to this poetic evocation of situation and character we have to
go back to certain passages in *Seven Poor Men of Sydney* and *The
Beauties and Furies*. Once again whiteness is the dominant motif
used to suggest experience beyond the common range, the bizarre
or the threatening. On Letty's first visit the nocturnal landscape is

bathed in intense moonlight; unable to sleep she "listened to soft
sounds in the moon-washed grass; animals, scurrying feet, ghosts
of animals, animals the Indians had known?" (pp. 317–18).
Haunting the huge house too, especially at night, is the presence
of the lanky, faintly repulsive Lucy. On Letty's second visit the
landscape is under snow and an air of desolation and death surrounds the house given over to Christmas festivities. The atmosphere created in these scenes is both a force acting on Letty and a
reflection of the emotional disturbance she is suffering. For parallels outside of Christina Stead's work we may think of Lawrence's
use of whiteness in a symbolist manner in *The Rainbow* and
Women in Love. There are hints also in *Letty Fox* of the black-
white antithesis that operates in *Seven Poor Men of Sydney;* Luke
Adams, whom Lucy is bound by temperament to hate, is the dark
Lawrentian male to whom Letty, escaping from Arnhem, goes to
allay her passion, the fox tearing at her vitals (p. 330).

Imperfect *Letty Fox* may be but, as the above instances show,
it contains good things. Some of its critics have remained
strangely insensitive to these, while others have exaggerated the
difficulties it creates for the reader.[10] It is, in fact, more readable
and more enjoyable than the next novel, *A Little Tea, a Little
Chat*.

XII *Another Picture of Life in New York*

Like *Letty Fox* this is a satire on the New York scene but the
time span is shorter and it focuses, in its picture of Robert Grant,
on the business world and those who inhabit its shady fringes. *A
Little Tea, a Little Chat* is a kind of sequel to *Letty Fox* in its
exploration of another side to life in New York, but not in its
choice of protagonist. Letty is a girl of many loves, sensual, head-
strong and foolish, but she is neither a true libertine like Grant,
nor a calculating harpy like the blondine, though she may seem to
the superficial observer to have much in common with both of
them.

The book opens in New York, April, 1941. Robert Grant, usually called Robbie, is a shrewd, ruthless, middle-aged businessman
who for years has made easy money as a cotton speculator and
dealer. He lives apart from wife and family and when not engaged in business spends his time in pursuit of women, of all
classes, creeds, and colors. Early in the story he is introduced to

Barbara Kent, aged thirty-two, down on her luck and desperate for cash. He starts the relationship in the usual way by inviting her to his rooms for a little tea, a little chat; he christens her the "blondine," installs her in a fashionable hotel, and before long imagines he is in love with her. But Barbara, with an eye for alimony, marries Adams, an army man; later she goes to Reno along with her mother and her friend Paula, all at Grant's expense, for her divorce and then starts urging Grant to divorce his wife and marry her.

War breaks out, Barbara disappears for a time and Grant traces her to Washington. He develops the idea that, because she has a European background, she may be a spy and so he pays a business acquaintance Hugo March to get confidential reports on her from a contact in the capital; he also employs a detective on his own account to keep watch on her. March keeps on extracting payments from Grant for furnishing him with fictitious reports, until Grant and his friend David Flack gradually realize they are being fooled. They set a trap for March and trick him into revealing his duplicity, and Grant now has the pleasure of devising a scheme of his own by means of which he bleeds March in return for the full $11,000 paid him. It turns out that Paula and Barbara have been in collusion with March all the time and, of course, have collected their percentages.

Grant takes up with Barbara again and a crowd of high-livers all out for a good time, but in February, 1943, she marries Churchill Downs, and Grant complains bitterly to the world of her deception. Throughout the course of his tangled relations with her, Grant pursues his normal life of lechery in town. At this point he consoles himself principally with one of his regulars, a married woman, Myra Coppelius, gets his elder son, Gilbert, an army officer, transferred to army film work, moves into a more expensive suite, and goes on acquiring property at home and abroad. Barbara returns to town and Grant learns he is being named as corespondent in a divorce suit to be brought against Downs. In the meantime Myra, realizing that Grant has broken all the promises he has made to her, commits suicide, and Gilbert begins to learn the truth about his father's evil ways. Barbara, threatening blackmail, continues to dun Grant for money. Ill feeling develops between father and son because Gilbert starts going with Celia Grimm, whom Robbie has in his sights. Barbara shrewdly takes

Grant's side in his quarrels with Gilbert and with the Flacks. In the end she gets her divorce from Downs and Grant foots the bill, thereby avoiding the public scandal he dreads.

Grant's life of shady business deals and loveless liaisons continues but he suddenly begins to feel old. Barbara gets hold of a document which vests his property in two corporations (owned by his sons) to avoid taxation. This means in effect that Gilbert owns outright three-quarters of his father's estate and could upset all Grant's plans by demanding his share. Now holding the trump card, Barbara moves into the basement apartment of one of Robbie's newly acquired Brooklyn houses. This is where Grant now lives, jealously guarding a hatbox of valuable documents, which he will not let out of his sight. He still goes to town each day but returns at night to Brooklyn, where he and Barbara live like an old married couple. It is here (in a manner to be described later) that he meets his fate. Barbara comes home to find him dead in the hall; she is tempted to clear out with the hatbox but decides to play safe, to ring the police and wait.

XIII   *The Character of Robert Grant*

This summary of the plot does not deal with all Robbie's women or all of his money-making activities, which include war profiteering; sufficient to say, his attitude to both is the same selfish opportunism—Grant is an Henri Léon with the endearing qualities left out. This means not that he is non-human but that he is repulsive as well as sinful and so has no claims on the reader's sympathy. He is a type that obviously has fascinated the novelist and he is taken apart here with a remorseless efficiency. *A Little Tea, a Little Chat* is held on a tighter rein than *Letty Fox;* it has the concentration and singleness of purpose that *Letty Fox* lacks, yet it is not as good a book.

Robbie Grant is the most thoroughgoing scoundrel in the whole of Christina Stead's gallery of modern rogues, and the least attractive. Jules Bertillon fleeced people on a grander scale, but he had charm, a genuine sense of humor, was capable of friendship and generosity. Grant is equally self-centered, but mean into the bargain. We might forgive him his ruthlessness in business—he is merely one cut-throat among many—but not the trouble he takes to cultivate the favors of drab working-class girls who can bring him black-market stockings, or his shameful deception and exploitation of his faithful old housekeeper, Mrs. MacDonald. Grant's life, like his speech, has a torrential quality. He is full of schemes and tricks for making and saving money which he then regrets having to spend on the pleasures he constantly seeks. His whole life is a mad, manic whirl of activity. All this is to hide the truth he is afraid to face—that he is a fear-haunted man, hollow at the core.

It is in his personal relationships that Grant is most loathsome. He uses people without any regard for their feelings or their rights. He makes and breaks promises at will and, when it suits his pocket, ruins the lives of those who have loved and trusted him. He knows he is directly responsible for Myra Coppelius' death but he runs away for fear of being implicated, though in his "loneliness" he was at the time of her accident (suicide?) on his way to visit her at her hotel. When crossed he becomes vindictive—witness the malicious letter he writes to the sheriffs about Celia Grimm because Gilbert has accompanied her on a tour supporting Negro rights. He betrays the confidences of Livy Wright and buys up her own property, cheap. He even fleeces the abandoned Laura, whom he continually talks of as the great love of his life, leaving her to die miserably in Italy. Always a great talker Grant is never at a loss when it comes to self-justification. His full name, ironically, is Robert Owen Grant, which makes us think of another cotton man, true socialist and philanthropist. Grant boasts frequently of his socialist principles but this is a mere mouthing of platitudes, attending grog parties for radicals, proclaiming a belief in equality yet exhibiting vicious racial prejudice. When forced upon the defensive, as he occasionally is by the blondine, he becomes a self-pitying, whining sentimentalist who cries for the love and understanding that have been denied him. Grant has no pride, no dignity—only selfishness and fear for his reputation.

XIV *The Difficulties Posed by* A Little Tea, a Little Chat

A Little Tea, a Little Chat is an honest and intelligent book; it is perceptive in its presentation of character and unsparing in its depiction of a sick, money-grubbing society; it is packed with precise observation and the carefully accumulated details that give a novel its authenticity. There is no ambiguity here to tease the reader, no uncertainty in the point of view. But the fact remains that it is not an easy book to read, nor does it offer as much in the rereading as the other novels (with the possible exception of *The Beauties and Furies*). Somehow, it is all rather cold. Several things seem to contribute to this final effect.

The depraved man has been successfully treated in literature far more often than the good (who usually interests us less), so it is not simply the character of Grant that is to blame. More to the point is how Grant is presented both in himself and in his relationship with others. A writer engaged in any sort of demolition work has more chance of success if he entertains the reader at the same time. In *Gulliver's Travels* Swift mixes plain statement and outrageous comedy, the factual and the fantastic, in whatever proportions necessary for effective satire. *A Little Tea, a Little Chat*, which is clearly an exposure of vice and corruption, is severely realistic in approach. Christina Stead has allowed herself none of the liberties of the satiric fable but has relied on the accuracy of her account to express her criticism. It is surprising that her flair for sardonic comedy (most appropriate to the subjects she is treating here) is not given freer play. When it does appear it is highly successful, as in Sections 45–47 where Mrs. Grant unexpectedly descends upon Robbie's New York hotel and the blondine coolly poses as a volunteer worker for the British War Relief Society until Livy Wright suddenly appears and the whole situation threatens to dissolve into some theatrical farce.

A Little Tea, a Little Chat might well have become a better book if Grant had been treated in a freer, comic vein. It is true, of course, that satire in the comic mode simplifies character in order to ridicule and chastise and that Christina Stead is making a serious character study of Grant. But, as fictional characters go, Grant is not a particularly complex figure, so there would be little loss if he were cut down to size. As it is, we come pretty soon to understand him, and the second half of the novel adds little to our knowledge. This seems one of the book's limitations—there is not enough to Grant to warrant the grilling he is given; we see through him easily and tend to lose interest. Furthermore, large slabs of the book are given to documenting his activities and his own speeches and, Grant being what he is, the effect is either repetitive (as in the accounts of his numerous liaisons) or prolonged (as in the intermittent story of his attempts to create a stage hit for Broadway).

Henri Léon, basically the same character as Grant, is created in the Falstaffian manner; the artistic delight comes through the character to the reader. Like Grant, Léon is a business rogue and a womanizer who is mean toward his women; but he is not made the center of a whole book. Furthermore, he has his redeeming features—loyalty, intelligence, even unselfishness in his dealings with his friends; he sins, but, like some Renaissance grandee, on a spectacular scale that calls for admiration. Robbie we can never admire. Of all the other large-scale portraits Crow is the most repulsive but, apart from the fact that he is not as bad as Grant, there are important differences. Crow's character gradually unfolds to Teresa and thereby retains the reader's interest. What is so compelling about him is that we first see him with Teresa's eyes, and in the early chapters, though a little odd, he is not altogether unattractive. We know too of his struggle to free himself from poverty and to find a niche in the academic world. His later cruel treatment of Teresa is psychologically convincing.

Furthermore, as a study in egoism Crow is all the more impressive because he is thrown into contrast with quite different people—with Quick who stands for true intelligence and warmth, and with Teresa herself for whom love is creative and liberating not merely the indulgence of whim. There are no characters strong enough in *A Little Tea, a Little Chat* to provide this sort of counterbalance to Grant and his kind. Mrs. Grant, Laura, Myra, the working-class girls, are Robbie's weakly protesting victims. The blondine and his business acquaintances are all tarred with the same brush as he; the Flacks, who alone seem capable of providing a different set of values to place against his, never quite assume this role effectively. This is the function they are apparently intended to have.

David Flack occasionally brings a fresh slant to our view of Robbie; more of this sort of thing would round out the character and make him more interesting. March and Flack are discussing Grant:

"The monkey always shies away from talking about the market. He don't join in; and there's this obsession about the blonde; he doesn't act like money to me."

"You forget, his father and mother were Europeans. Robbie has a lot of that in him. He doesn't talk about money because, first, he doesn't want you to know he has any; second, he sincerely thinks it's vulgar."

March said, "If it's an act, it's too deep for me."

Flack explained with excitement, "He loves luxury—to the luxurious, money is vulgar." (p. 90)

Gilbert provides some of the counterpoise the book needs. Being close to his father for the first time, he begins to realize what sort of man Robbie really is. He becomes bitter: " 'I'm the son of a woman with sleeping sickness and a man who puts on greasepaint to show better under the street lamps with whores' " (p. 332–33). But then Gilbert himself is more than a little boring. The reader endorses this judgment of him: "Gilbert was what Flack called 'a cold-blooded Hotspur' who was rationally intolerant, genially censorious, originally tedious" (p. 103).

XV   *The Relationship between Grant and the Blondine*

The most interesting part of *A Little Tea, a Little Chat* is the relationship between Grant and the blonde. She is important to him in a number of ways. She is the only woman tough enough to stand up to him and shrewd enough to manage him. Then, again, she seems to satisfy the other needs of his strange personality. Robbie must have the excitement and the challenge that his involvement with her provides. Her affairs with other men, her playing him for cash, her blackmail threats, are a source of interest and activity, and the first need of his nature is activity. Grant is the unhappy case of the libertine who finds little pleasure in his pleasures. The blondine, by resisting, breaks the pattern that habit has clamped upon him thereby offering a means of escape from himself.

Grant we understand only too well; the blondine, treated for the most part indirectly, presents some difficulties. We can rarely take her words at their face value; our assessment has to be built mainly out of Robbie's fluctuating opinions of her and by guessing about the game she is playing, mainly off-stage, with other men. Neither source is reliable, nor are the many rumors she inspires. She remains a rather mysterious character throughout, though her general aims are clear enough. She is sometimes allowed to speak freely, notably in Section 44 where she badgers Robbie for money and Section 46 where she puts pressure upon Gilbert, but such occasions are surprisingly rare. In the long run this elusiveness has its advantages; it reinforces the aloofness of the woman, which is perhaps what tantalizes Grant most of all.

XVI *Significance of the Conclusion*

The note of mystery is sounded again at the end. Old Hilbertson, who has scores to settle, comes unexpectedly upon the scene. He calls one day at the house and finds Barbara there alone. She is attracted to this stranger, tells him about the hatbox that Grant carries everywhere and accepts an invitation to meet him elsewhere on the Sunday. Hilbertson is thereby able to confront Grant alone. The scene is almost cryptic in its brevity:

At the door was a strong, bent old man with large eyes, intense as jewels.

"Hilbertson," said Grant.

"Not a bad memory. You remember what I said?"

"It's a great mistake, it was all a mistake," said Grant. The Sunday supplement fell from his hand, he stepped back without thinking. He became pale with fright.

"You're quite an old man now," said Hilbertson.

"You are old too," said Grant, but he gasped: he could hardly get the words out. He watched Hilbertson, whose hand was in his pocket. Suddenly, Grant fainted. Hilbertson looked a while and closed the door. (p. 393)

Behind this scene lurks the analogy with the death of Don Giovanni in the grip of the statue.[11] Hilbertson, like the Commendatore, arises out of the past to exact vengeance. Hilbertson's hand is in his pocket; Grant sees this and, afraid that Hilbertson is about to shoot him, collapses with a heart attack and dies. Thus his fears of dying alone in a private house come true (p. 180). And so *A Little Tea, a Little Chat* provides yet another parallel to *House of All Nations*. Both Léon and Grant fear Azrael; Léon is terrified by Julius Kratz as Grant is by Hilbertson; the two roles are linked with the notion of death, the avenging angel.[12] And in *Scene Five* of *House of All Nations* ("Small Kratz and Great Léon") we find Léon described as "a Don Juan in the grain trade" (p. 59). Léon, too, finally meets his match in a blonde. *A Little Tea, a Little Chat* would be inferior to Christina Stead's best work if only for the reason that some of its basic material has already been covered in *House of All Nations.*

XVII   *Style and Dialogue*

The style of *A Little Tea, a Little Chat* calls for brief comment. In the account of *Letty Fox* already quoted from, Christina Stead refers, accurately, to her next book as "very frank, but written in an austere style." The color and richness of the prose in the early books has given way now to a spare and chill monochrome. Dialogue predominates, however, and some of this has the idiomatic vigor that gives continual force to the books from *House of All Nations* onward. But only some. Grant is the stumbling block again. He is a compulsive talker and when speaking in character, as he is most of the time, he can be tedious. Realism has its disadvantages. Here is a typical example:

"If I don't like you, you don't get a penny. It's my money. Never mind what I promise. I promise here, I promise there, if I see a good thing, if I believe in a man. You bring me something and you'll get your money, subject to my approval and you'll sign for it, and you'll take it all on your own responsibility and not come to me for it afterwards; I'm clean about money, I don't pay twice. You got to respect my money. If it weren't for my money you'd be a laborer, a workman in a mill or a whitecollar man in an office with no brains and no chance. You're Grant's son. I'm not saying that to insult you, my boy; I don't consider it an insult. All right, you can't make money. Everyone can't." (pp. 364–65)

Occasionally Grant rises above this level and is more interesting to listen to, but when he does he sounds more like Jules Bertillon than the real Robbie. " 'John Stuart Mills and Albert Spencer said, if you gave a penny to a blind beggar, you destroyed the foundations of society, or to a man who plays *Il Trovatore* on the hurdygurdy, you destroy the foundations of art and artists; that's a serious thought. I'm a laissez-faire. You can't patch up all the holes in the social fabric' " (p. 342).

XVIII   *Communal Life*

The last book of this American trio, *The People with the Dogs*, though less arresting in its characters and situations, has strong claims to be rated the best. It is of particular importance in a general study of Christina Stead's work because it explores fresh material in an unexpected vein. *The People with the Dogs* by contrast with *A Little Tea, a Little Chat* is gentle, even affectionate, in its approach to the main group of characters. It is a mellow novel, steeped in humor not (for the most part) the acid or sardonic variety that Christina Stead usually commands, but, as in the description of Whitehouse, the Massines' old country estate, the humor of pure enjoyment and acceptance. *The People with the Dogs* has been described by the author as a book not about the American stereotypes that most people know of from foreign and from fashionable American writings, but about a sort of Cherry Orchard family, descendants of nineteenth-century Russian liberals.

The Massines are a pleasant, cultured, eccentric tribe, with a touch of old world Bohemianism, lavishing affection upon their pets, and out of contact with modern life. A novel about such people is not likely to generate strong feelings unless the characters are to be slaughtered satirically and there is no question of that treatment here. *The People with the Dogs* cannot, therefore, be expected to match the intensities of *The Man Who Loved Children* and *For Love Alone*. Jose Yglesias describes it, fairly enough, as a charming book which "occupies that lovable place in her work that *A Room with a View* does in E. M. Forster's cannon."[13]

To one who has read Christina Stead closely the central concern of *The People with the Dogs* is not altogether unexpected. *Seven Poor Men of Sydney* takes account of the political and social movements of the 1920's and their theoretical background, and the subsequent novels all show a similar awareness of public affairs. One of the writer's interests, hinted at here and there, is the notion of the ideal community, Fourier's system for the reorganization of society through the socialistic phalanx. The restless, idealistic Teresa talks about marriage at the age of fourteen and community houses where the young, separated from their parents, should learn from scientists and the best artists and writers. She even says love should be taught so that the young will make no mistakes. Sam Pollit's ideas include the phalanstery both within his own family and then as part of his great plan for the reorganization of society according to the most enlightened scientific and humanitarian principles. And Emily Howard, the central character in a novel only part of which has so far been published, says " 'Family love is the only true selfless love; it's natural communism.'

That is the origin of our feeling for communism: to each according to his needs, from each according to his capacity; and everything is arranged naturally, without codes and without policing.' " [14]

The People with the Dogs turns from such theorizings to recreate in the Massines what remains after World War II of a nineteenth-century attempt at communal living at the country estate of Whitehouse. Here on land left by Edward's grandfather for the purpose there is a roof for everyone (family and friends) and all claims are equal. Whitehouse is the muddled, happy, down-at-heel "Massine Republic" to which most of the family who do not already live there repair for the summer. It is a backwater in modern American life but even Edward, a confirmed Manhattan dweller who loves to roam the city streets, feels its pull. The book concerns his attempts to break the apathy the past seems to lay upon him and to find a new direction. The most important of the older generation is Edward's aunt Oneida Solway, whose name recalls one of the best known nineteenth-century religious societies, the Oneida Community, originally strictly Communistic but later modifying its attitude toward family life and property.[15]

Once again Christina Stead writes a book whose social picture requires a large number of characters and this could lead a hasty reader to repeat the old criticism that she has no grasp of form. Such a view seems to be supported by the absence of a strong plot. But *The People with the Dogs* is in fact a well-constructed novel built on a set of character groupings and inter-relationships instead of the dramatic ordering of incidents. Little enough happens as we follow the hero's apparently aimless wanderings from place to place, but Edward is changing slowly and the book charts this progress. The detail is more economically used than in *Letty Fox* and the consequence is a firmer control and a greater unity of effect.

XIX   *The Story*

Part One shows us Edward Massine's life in Lower Manhattan, "the last of gaslight New York." Edward owns two adjoining houses inherited from his parents, and gets his income from rents. An army sergeant during the war, now aged thirty-three, he is kind, easy-going and lazy. Though he has known his girl Margot for eleven years he has never been able to take the plunge into marriage. Like all the Massines he loves animals and is devoted to his cat Westfourth (who occupies the front room in his flat) and his dog Musty. Margot berates him for his fear of marriage. " 'You can't let a dog suffer, dear good Edward, but you can twist the soul of a human being' " (p. 85). He feels he ought to do something positive, such as fighting against the threat of atomic war, but he cannot bestir himself. The Massines prepare for the summer at Whitehouse but Edward just wants to stay in town. He finds himself, by accident, marching in a May Day procession and, to his surprise, gets a thrill out of it. He is finally persuaded to go to Whitehouse to attend the marriage there of two of his childhood playmates.

Part Two describes the old Home Farm and the colony of relatives, friends and tenants occupying the various dwelling places on the property. Life goes on amid family gossiping and quarrels, to the accompaniment of music-making, the preparation for the wedding, and the continual antics of the dogs who seem to take the place of young children. The farm tenants are discontented with the decay of the property, and the various problems growing out of the entanglements between the Massines and the friends who occupy land on the estate are so great that Edward despairs of establishing any kind of order. He cannot decide about Margot, tries to write to her but fails to do even that. Oneida and Victor-Alexander, a dapper old bachelor once favored by Oneida's parents as her husband, quarrel bitterly. Edward, significantly, is much moved by the wedding ceremony. The celebrations are helped on by two carloads of morons (from a home for the feeble-minded) whom Dan Barnes has brought along from his factory for an outing.

Part Three. In mid-August Edward (who came to Whitehouse for three days and has stayed three months) hastens back to town on learning that Margot is about to marry another man. To his surprise he fails to prevent the marriage and the next day suddenly returns to Whitehouse where he can be happy again.

Part Four is "Whitehouse in Autumn." Edward stays on until the ailing Westfourth dies and can be buried near the other pets. Victor-Alexander, who for years has shut himself off from the world in "Solitude," the house he built on Massine land, is forced by the sowthistle to pull down his high garden walls and now proposes that he run the whole property as farm tenant overlord. Edward just laughs and relaxes, but back in New York finds himself at a dead-end. He has now lost both his pets (Oneida has taken Musty) and Margot: " 'I have too little to do, but nothing attracts me' " (p. 258).

In *Part Five* Edward goes to stay with middle-aged friends, Philip Christy and his sister Nell, once enthusiastic anarchists, who now live in the Harlem slums. Here he sinks into another kind of life. He is afraid to pursue his affair with the singer Vera Sarine, but finds some interest in the project of writing the memoirs of a gun moll whom he and Philip have met. He is still not sure if he is turning his back on life. A family crisis forces him into activity of a different kind. Philip is knocked down by a trolley when trying to save his ailing whippet, Lady, and dies. Nell, broken-hearted, takes to bed to starve herself to death. Edward tends her, is awakened to compassion and succeeds in winning her back to life again. Having been forced into responsibility he now looks forward to marriage and a life of his own.

The final section is called "New Configurations." Vera, who puts her career before marriage, is to go abroad and Edward develops a love for the actress Lydia, who gradually comes to replace Vera in his affections. He bids farewell to Vera, plucks up courage to propose to Lydia, and is accepted. Later he introduces her as his wife to the Massine tribe. Unknown to Oneida he plans to get away from New York and Whitehouse to work on a new play for Lydia.

XX   *The Character of Edward*

The account of Edward in New York reveals him as a kind of twentieth-century Oblomov always seeking to avoid decisions and purposeful activity. He occupies his time pleasantly enough, sleeping much of the day, following his theatrical interests, visiting friends, chatting with his tenants, and walking the city streets with Musty. He is a dilettante just discontented enough to feel he ought to be doing something more satisfying and useful. He is aware of other responsibilities but temperament, habit, and an adequate income confirm him in his indolence. Christina Stead views his plight sympathetically, for Edward is greatly superior to those hard, selfish New Yorkers who throng the pages of *A Little Tea, a Little Chat*. When Edward tells his cousin Walt that he

feels he ought to go out and fight for some cause, Walt replies,
" 'Fighting for freedom is not a matter of sentiment but necessity.
Anyone who expects causes and wretched suffering peoples to
save his soul ends up a traitor. Living the way you are you can't
possibly betray anyone. A man isn't a sister of charity'" (p. 93).
Walt puts the case for him far better than he could himself in a
defense of the Massine way of life which blends irony with approval.

"You only understand the communal life, that's why you don't want
to marry, isn't it? You don't see the reason for crawling into a corner
with one woman and having one child. You need abundant multiple
life around you like Whitehouse, like the Massines; the perfect still
life, eh? Ha-ha. Fruitfulness with grapes and rabbits dropping over
the edges of an oak table on a woven cloth—and many dogs and
dishes and many children and many days? Isn't that you funda-
mentally? You run a lodginghouse, you run a community. You're married to many! Ha-ha-ha. Lucky man. You're all right, Ned. And all
without any theory, Anarchist, Socialist, what-have-you, just the Massine Bill of Rights. You're born in the Golden Age just because old
Dad Massine established the Fiftieth State of the Union, the Massine
Enclave, with the following sweet words: 'I leave Whitehouse to
furnish a roof for you all, rich, poor, working, idle. All will be free on
the Home Farm to do as they like.' What has happened, Edward? You
are all the friends of Man. In God's name, what more do you want
out of life than to be such a man?" (p. 94)

Edward is encouraged by all this to attempt a self-assessment:
" 'Do you know, I am not as lost as I make out. My state of mind
can be called undefined hesitant anticipation'" (p. 95).

XXI *The Power of Whitehouse*

At Whitehouse, the huge wild hops vine, which threatens to
take over completely, strangling everything that comes within its
range, becomes the potent symbol of all that Edward has inherited, the past that holds him in its grip:

It held, embraced, but did not crush the ground, the house, and all
there brought by dogs and men: bones, sheathed copper wire needed
for watering the cows, old leather shoes hidden by a predecessor of
the Abbot, a sadiron, and all the things lost by this fertile careless
family, and all the things loved by this productive, abundant family

for seventy years; the deep ineradicable cables plunging into the hill
soil and sending up at great distances their wires and threads; and the
whole family and house and barns and the home-acres, in the great
throttling of the twining vine. It tore away easily, leaving all the growing roots there. In a few days, the injured roots completed their repairs
and sent up a new line of roots and leaves and the work of monopoly
went on. (p. 151)

XXII   *The Pattern of Casual Events*

It is only when back in town that he ever seems likely to free
himself of Whitehouse's tentacles. Bewildered by Margot's marriage Edward drifts about till he ends up at the house of his
friends, the Blocks. Dorothy and Waldemar are puppet-makers,
German by birth. Waldemar (like George Haller in *House of All
Nations*) is such a gourmand that the Blocks can afford to eat only
on certain days. The day Edward calls happens to be an occasion
for eating and so he is invited to the feast. This curious scene
seems at first mere indulgence on the author's part, but it turns
out to be one of a number of experiences Edward now has that
combine to drive him back to Whitehouse again. Whenever puppets appear in this novel they symbolize Edward's attachment to
the unreal. The Blocks, moreover, are exiles and the reader is entitled to see them as prototypes of what Edward Massine might
have become. Excited by the food and wine Waldemar talks at
great length about his early life in Europe, his political insight, and
his aspirations. But the fact remains that he has never been anything except a toymaker. After this Edward calls on his friend
Sam Innings. Sam, as usual, is crying (like some hopeless character in Chekov) over a woman, the beloved Vera, who wants nothing to do with him; another failure—this time one who has not the
courage to go for the woman he wants. Edward then collects Al
Burrows, the pharmacist, and the two of them visit the Turkish
baths. Here occurs one of those vivid vignettes that are scattered
through Christina Stead's fiction. Edward is revolted by the sight
of grossly fat women sitting round half naked in one of the steam-
ing assembly rooms, their shopping bags bulging with food, playing cards and telling outrageously filthy stories. Soon afterward he
feels a desire for Whitehouse again and the clear air of upland
valleys and high mountains. Even more significant is the interlude

with the Christys, which occupies the whole of *Part Five*, "Scratch Park."

Philip, a skilful optician, is still a man of great charm and generosity but disenchanted, a failure and a drunkard. Like a Massine, Philip loves his dog; in fact his love goes further than the Massines', for he loses his life trying to save her—whether drunk at the time or not we cannot be sure though the devoted Nell, of course, maintains he was sober. The ironies multiply here. Phil is the ex-idealist doting on his Lady, who seems to mean more to him than sister or mistress; Nell in self-reproach elects to die, her humanitarian friends endorsing her decision on the grounds of principle; and Edward must assert the priorities of human love and obligation.

At this point we may recall the murder of the woman near Edward's home in the first section of the novel, a deed which then made no impression on him and his friends. Now it is death (and the death-wish in Nell) that brings Edward out of himself, that, paradoxically, awakens him to life. In such apparently casual episodes in the wandering narrative of these two sections there are patterns of personal relationships which dramatize with unobtrusive skill the book's central concerns. Edward is now happy just to live; he puts Lydia before Musty and, avoiding the fate of hapless Sam, takes the initiative and wins a wife. He has sense enough also to get away from Whitehouse for a time, at least, but, though anxious to begin a new life, he still cannot bear to see the Massine Republic disappear. His final plea is Chekovian in its recognition of the inevitability of change and its desire to preserve the humaneness of the past: "' . . . will you change the Republic of Arts and Letters and Humane Sloth? Why there with a little good will and mutual aid and sensible mild nonchalance, with live and let live, we take vacations from the epoch of wars and revolutions! Oh, keep Musty away. My soul! Must we be efficient too? I would rather have the vine'" (p. 343). The other members of the family do not know which vine he means, so unaware are they of the implications of the lives they lead.

XXIII   *The Novelist's Sympathy for Her Characters*

Oneida is the most important character of the older generation, and the way she feels about dogs helps to explain the Massines in

general and to define Christina Stead's attitude toward them.
Oneida drools over Madame X before the operation, as if the dog
were a favorite child. The discussion at the veterinary's house
comes back again and again to family pets of the past. Oneida
is on edge and quick to defend the whole canine race:

"Jeff was devoted to us. Do you remember when he dug up a whole
warren of little rabbits and brought them all as a present. That morning the whole slope was literally covered with bunnies. He was a very
loving dog." "Ugh!" said Lady. "Why? Those rabbits only try to decoy
the dogs down the hole so that they'll suffocate to death. I hate
them. They're little devils," said Oneida. (pp. 48–49)

When the excited pack of dogs snap and bark around the terrified
grocer's boy at Whitehouse Edward yells at Oneida to call them
off and she replies: " 'They're innocent, they think they're pro-
tecting us' " (p. 136). She reproves the unfortunate lad: " 'They're
only dawgs. Aren't you ashamed to be frightened of dogs? They
can smell it. It's adrenalin in your blood' " (p. 134). (The whole
of the long opening section of *Part Two* is a riotous comedy in
which the leading roles are played by dogs, whose separate
identities emerge with startling clarity as the scene develops—
Abbot, an irrepressible young terrier is the star performer and
once he starts on his early morning rounds anything can happen.)
It comes as no surprise when we learn later that as a young
woman Oneida once attended a seance at Victor-Alexander's and
when asked if she wished to speak to anyone in the beyond
named her darling little Picky, a crossbred mongrel who had
died three years before.
    But Oneida is clearly no fool, even where her affections are in-
volved, and is able to talk of her beloved animals with some detachment (p. 175). She knows that dogs are her substitute for
children, but her love for animals has not destroyed her capacity
for loving people too. When she senses that Edward's relationship for Lydia has reached a crucial stage she can reprove her
sister-in-law for harping on the death of Madame X, Oneida's beloved bull-terrier: " 'Oh . . . let's forget that dead dog; let's come
down to earth. What does Edward mean?' " (p. 332). As she
nurses the aging Musty she says she will have no more dogs but
henceforth will given all her love to husband Lou. But, like Ed-

ward, she still has links with the past as the book ends. We glimpse her finally in great excitement over Edward's marriage and a new pup Lou has given her.

The comedy of *The People with the Dogs* grows from the wry compassion with which Christina Stead views her characters. There is a certain irony of situation in the insulated life the Massines live in a hustling, go-ahead, materialistic world. But Christina Stead's treatment of them never becomes the satiric exposure that marks *Letty Fox* and *A Little Tea, a Little Chat*. *The People with the Dogs*, so different in many respects from her first novel, shows the same feeling for the lives of the humble and the obscure which made Joseph the most sympathetically presented character of *Seven Poor Men of Sydney*.

The indolent Edward is not created with the richness and depth that transform the Russian Oblomov from a lazy man into a great tragi-comic figure, but then Edward is not himself the reason for the novel that is built around him. He is a Massine with one foot in the post-war world and his real function is to give focus and depth to the picture of the Massine Republic. *The People with the Dogs* has a Chekovian air; it treats groups rather than individuals, and looks with affection upon a segment of society which, in the nature of things, must change. It raises the question: Will the Massines just disappear or will they and their way of life survive the assaults and the neglect of the modern world? Not the least of the book's achievements is the way it poses this question.

first volume of stories since *The Salzburg Tales,* but the shortest
of the four, "The Dianas," is a good deal longer than any of the
Tales, and the longest, "Girl from the Beach," runs to some 130
pages of manuscript. It is not surprising that in any venture outside the full-scale novel Christina Stead should at this stage in
her career turn to the long rather than the short story. Her central interest has always been the study of character; this interest
has increased over the years and is the dominant feature of *The
Puzzleheaded Girl.* The psychological scrutiny is closer and more
sustained than in any of the early tales and the stories accordingly become longer and more complex.

Even "The Right-Angled Creek," subtitled "A sort of ghost
story," rich in atmospheric evocation of place and season in the
hill country of Delaware, is memorable for its characterization
too. Primarily it creates a sense of place (and its effect on different
kinds of people) and of the pressure of past upon present, but it
also brings off a fine study of a writer living in the constant fear of
the alcoholism which has hung over his whole life. The other
three stories are character studies of Americans, both at home and
abroad, done with great verve and deadly skill by a writer who
knows perfectly the kind of people she is depicting and the artistic
and moral effects she wants.

Each story in its turn goes beyond the presentation of individual character to further implication or thematic statement. "The
Puzzleheaded Girl" is a picture of a strangely innocent, self-pos-
sessed yet bewildered woman, Honor Lawrence, who seems
doomed to wander the world, never achieving, perhaps never
wanting love or a home. Her image haunts the businessman Debrett, who befriends her as a young girl and cannot avoid feeling
sympathy for her even when she proves a nuisance. He himself
takes courage from her and becomes a traveller in search of a
better life. Despite the curious muddle of her existence Debrett
continues to believe in her essential purity and honesty. Mari's
attempt to sum her up after news of her death is, at best, only
partly convincing:

"She's the ragged, wayward heart of woman that doesn't want to be
caught and hasn't been caught," said Mari, in her beautiful, metallic
voice. "She never was in love." He looked at her in doubt. "She never
loved anyone," said Mari. Debrett thought of this: he did not believe

it; but walking up and down under the trees in someone's garden he bent his head a little, saw nothing, wiped his eyes with his hands.[1]

"The Dianas" and "Girl from the Beach" are both studies of Americans in Paris (mainly) and New York in the immediate postwar years. They dramatize conflicts of values and national differences with a wealth of detail and acute social observation. "Girl from the Beach" has some splendid comic scenes, whose lash is as sharp as ever. Whereas "The Puzzleheaded Girl" depends chiefly on nuance and implication, "Girl from the Beach" is notable for the brilliance of its scenes and the vigor of its characterization. Its central figures are middle-aged George Paul, a restless, pushing, freelance journalist, who has a flair for falling in love with young girls, and Linda Hill, a "normal girl" from New York who gets into the most amazing muddles in Europe and yet in her babyish way comes through them all safely. George's divorced wife, the irrepressible Barby, is unforgettable; so too is the exquisite miniature of Prince Dmitri, liar and sponger, who, nursing an ivory model of a female hand (which he persuades Linda is a copy of his beloved wife's), might be some crazy character from Jacobean melodrama who has wandered into the grotesque wasteland of twentieth-century comedy.

The heroines of both "The Dianas" and "Girl from the Beach" are rootless, empty-headed young women living in a civilized (and corrupt) society which they cannot begin to understand. They are both obsessed with the idea of marriage and terrified of sex; they are emotionally immature and have father fixations which lead them to toy with and then refuse the affections of the middle-aged Americans to whom they turn in place of younger men. Lydia, like her mother Hester, is a twittering flirt, a huntress. "She had a fleet motion always as if running, with the feet arched, slightly bent forward." Ironically, Hester triumphed over the positive, dominant Diana in the chase for the same man. Aunt Diana remains a spinster and tries to lure Lydia from a loyalty to her mother, but to no avail. Back home Lydia drifts through to marriage and money. This story was mangled when published by the *Saturday Evening Post* under the changed title of "The Huntress." In the course of abridgement most of the uncomplimentary references to Americans abroad and certain passages central to the characterization of the heroine were omitted. The result is a story which would upset no one, but which is a pale and gutless version of the original.

II *Recent Projects and* Dark Places of the Heart

The Puzzleheaded Girl is a book which should have an immediate appeal and a favorable critical reception, its virtues and achievements are so clear. Christina Stead's latest novel, *Dark Places of the Heart,* is a different proposition. It is a more ambitious work which, if the early American reviews are any guide, is going to worry some of its readers. It will appear in England under the title the author first chose for it, *Cotters' England.*

The long gap between the last two novels turns out to be no cause for concern at all. In addition to a substantial amount of translating in the early 1950's Christina Stead has been working consistently at her fiction; it is only now that some of the fruits are becoming available. *The Puzzleheaded Girl* and *I'm Dying Laughing* are products of this period and there is other material in various stages of readiness. *Dark Places of the Heart,* only just published, was in all essentials finished more than ten years ago; it happened to be one of those books delayed by rewriting and for other reasons. It has been worth waiting for. It shows Christina Stead in full command of her powers and as original as ever.

The central character is Nellie Cook (née Cotter) from a working-class family in England's industrial north, driven to revolt in her youth by a thirst for knowledge and excitement and by a desire to serve the cause of the downtrodden, and now, in middle age working for a newspaper in London. Her house, in a scruffy suburb, becomes a dwelling place for the various women she collects and insists on helping. Scrawny, restless, loquacious, self-tormented Nellie is a friendly tyrant with an incurable passion for interfering in the lives of others—nearly always with fatal effect. Her husband George, a life-long labor man, now spends much of his time abroad on international missions and Nellie's life is given more to controlling the affairs of her unfortunate "chicks" and "pets" and her wayward brother Tom than to her frustrating work as journalist for a socialist paper. Nellie is a lesbian, and, for all her political activities, a Bohemian with no intellectual grasp of political or social affairs. She is a would-be revolutionary, a protester of freedom imprisoned by her shallow, histrionic, domineering, self-indulgent nature; an odd, rather repellent woman, but a wonderfully vital character and thoroughly consistent in all her strangeness.

Dark Places of the Heart approaches, in its own way, certain of the subjects Christina Stead has dealt with in earlier books—notably sham socialism and the brother-sister relationship. A good many of her characters are people who attach themselves (if only in speech) to the radical cause; the Folliots, Catherine Baguenault, Mendelssohn, Tom Winter, Oliver Fenton, Sam Pollit, Alphendéry, Robbie Grant, Flack, Phil Christy, and several of the secondary characters in *House of All Nations* and *Letty Fox.* And of these more than a few are failures or betrayers of one kind or another. Toward the end of *The Beauties and Furies* Elvira says: " 'It's hateful being a bourgeois. I really went with Oliver because I didn't think he was a bourgeois. But he's just the new bourgeois, the nervous shying one who has to talk sham-socialism' " (p. 363). The would-be revolutionaries of *The Beauties and Furies* find their (very different) counterparts in the lapsed socialists of *Dark Places of the Heart.* In both books the immediate focus of attention is individual character and personal relationships, but the political theme, often submerged in the early novel, is much more adroitly and tellingly handled in *Dark Places of the Heart.*

The brother-sister relationship, as in *Seven Poor Men of Sydney,* becomes one of the central concerns of the novel. With it is associated the recurring imagery of the mirror and the dance in the hall of mirrors. This metaphor is used to suggest the sense of unreality that underlies the close relationship between Nellie and Tom. Tom has been formed partly in her image and this makes him a kind of shadow character like Michael Baguenault. For all his charm and his deep love of England and its past, as reflected in the countryside, Tom is strangely cold and, apparently, will always be an incomplete man hoping to find a woman who can give fulness to his life. Both he and Nellie have the savior streak. Most of the direct analyses of their relationship come from Nellie herself, as she continually tries to prevent Tom from taking up with other women. She sees herself attached to reality and Tom to the shadow. But there is more trustworthy evidence to suggest that the unreality is not all on Tom's side. Eliza, who knew the Cotters in the early days, used to feel there was something not quite human about Tom and Nellie, "the fatal brother and sister." One of the book's key scenes is that in which they dance together in the distorting Palace of Mirrors at a country side-show. In the curious association that involves Tom, Marion, and the other two men who have a place in Marion's life, there occurs, in the different form of make-believe, the half-brother and half-sister relationship which exists in real life between Michael and Catherine in *Seven Poor Men of Sydney*.

III *Working-Class England*

Although *Dark Places of the Heart* focuses on Nellie, its central concern is the larger one that emerges through and beyond her—Cotters' England, working-class England as it is, and so different from what it might have been. As one perceptive critic has said, Christina Stead is asking (in a novelistic way) why the English working class has not made the revolution and he goes on: "Though she deals only with its fringes and does not go to the center of its trade union, Labour Party and intellectual circles, she has recreated the full ambience of its opportunism, charlatanism and demoralization. Her unspoken judgment is as harsh as the explicit ones of Balzac, Proust, Joyce; unlike them, however, she does not base her critique on the better life of another age, or turn inward or withdraw or become nostalgic." [2] And it is a measure of her objectivity that in the process she creates such an incisive and unsentimental picture of working class customs, beliefs, and attitudes in her account of the Cotter household in Bridgehead. It is the same cool sympathy which enables us to understand the attraction of the Jago group for young Nellie and her friends, and to endorse the novelist's account of failure and betrayal made inescapable by ignorance, the appeal of nostrums and the lures of personal gratification.

Dark Places of the Heart is not that mythical creature, the perfect novel. It has the casual, surprising contours, the shocks, the meandering movement of life itself; in places it is repetitive and Nellie, especially in her nagging of Tom about Marion, is sometimes tedious. At the same time it is a book rich in insight and full of a disturbing power. One of its remarkable achievements is the convincing way it blends the commonplace and the strange; the realistic and the grotesque, which lie in uneasy partnership in the early books, are now fused into a single vision. There is no better example of this than the brief but unforgettable climax in which Nellie clad in Tom's cast-off airman's suit, beckons Caroline from her bedroom into the attic to observe the grotesque scene of feminine riot in the moonlit backyard below.

IV Characterization, the True Center

This study has attempted to show that Christina Stead's work has both the substance and artistic merit that some have denied her. It has traced the development of her fiction from the stylistic exuberances and the fantasy of her first books through the intellectual passion of *House of All Nations* down to the more consistent naturalism of the novels of the American group. In the course of time her overriding concern with character has become more and more obvious. It is an interest in a man for what he is, a mysteriously unique creature (unexceptional though he may appear to the world) and for what he becomes in his immediate relations with others and society at large. This interest underlies even the youthful intensities and rhetoric of *Seven Poor Men of Sydney*, so that when Edwin Muir describes most of the characters in this book as "frustrated men and women of genius" it seems that he has been carried away by what he calls Christina Stead's "visionary imaginative power" into overlooking their basic, ordinary humanity.[3] They are not geniuses of any kind, but fairly common types of people given a capacity for expressing themselves more intensely than in real life. Michael, the most abnormal of the main characters, is, to put it clinically, a schizoid temperament and there are plenty of his type around if it comes to counting heads.

V The Question of Real and Unreal Characters

Christina Stead has said "the object of the novel is characterization"[4] and she is in this sense a thoroughly traditional novelist, even though her early work was not always naturalistic in its approach. She clearly believes the novelist's task is to present people as they really are—and in ways that will make them acceptable to her readers. Yet the most common criticism of her work (apart from its alleged lack of form) is that, for all her great talents, she does not possess the essential gift of the realistic novelist, the capacity for creating thoroughly credible characters or, as it is sometimes put, "the ability to create character in the round." This criticism, it is true, has been applied mainly to the early books but exception is sometimes taken to the characters in the novels after *House of All Nations* also. Such a judgment cannot be conclusively proved or disproved. The reader must finally decide for himself. It should be observed, however, that critics have always been prone to this particular way of condemning novels. Dickens and Dostoevsky were taken to task on this account and their achievements were so great that one begins to suspect that the charge is often all too facile and misleading.

In the critic's vocabulary "credible," "real," and "lifelike" may mean no more than "ordinary," "average," and "within the limits of my observation." Charged with creating caricatures instead of describing "real" people Dickens once said the fault lay perhaps not in his pictures but in the inability of others to see what was in front of their eyes. On another occasion, defending fantasy, he wrote: "It does not seem to me to be enough to say of any description that it is the exact truth. The exact truth must be there; but the merit or art in the narrator, is the manner of stating the truth. As to which thing in literature, it always seems to me that there is a world to be done." [5] Dostoevsky, for his part, had strong views on common beliefs as to what constituted the unreal and the incredible:

What most people regard as fantastic and lacking in universality, I hold to be the inmost essence of truth. Arid observation of everyday trivialities I have long since ceased to regard as realism—it is quite the reverse. In any newspaper one takes up, one comes across reports of wholly authentic facts, which nevertheless strike one as extraordinary. Our writers regard them as fantastic, and take no account of them; and yet they are the truth, for they are facts.[6]

Certain reviewers of fiction in our day would do well to ponder these words and, furthermore, to accept the postulate that there is little point in writing a novel unless you have something special and unusual to say. To the disapproving reader who cannot accept the money-making maniacs of *House of All Nations* as credible one can only retort, "You have no respect for facts outside your own experience and no idea of the overwhelming power of human obsession." The objection to Christina Stead's characterization may well be to her way of looking at people, to her insistence on their capacity to surprise the casual or conventional observer.

VI   *The Corrupt City*

The world of Christina Stead's fiction is neither a cosy nor a comforting one, but it is certainly the twentieth century seen at a sharp angle of vision and with an unflinching honesty. In his autobiographical *The Roaring Twenties,* Jack Lindsay speaks of the Australian poet Chris Brennan and his grasp of the divided nature of man "in the post-Baudelairean world of the cash-nexus and the city desert." [7] The modern city, money, and the lack of money are recurring subjects in Christina Stead's work. They are present from the start in *Seven Poor Men of Sydney.* Above the filth and despair of the slums there comes to Mendelssohn an occasional vision of hope and enlightenment, but the other characters are, for the most part, typical of Christina Stead's wanderers in the city deserts of the modern world; Joseph and Withers, Catherine and Michael tramp the streets of Sydney as if searching for a way out of their troubles. So too Teresa becomes a wanderer, though a clear purpose gives her strength to endure ill-health and poverty. *House of All Nations* is dominated by Paris, its banks, and the power of international finance, which threatens public and private life alike. Adam Constant's denunciation reminds us of Balzac's view of Paris as expounded by Vautrin using the image of the jungle in his speech to the young Eugène in *Père Goriot.* The corrupt city figures in the later books too, notably in *Letty Fox* and *A Little Tea, a Little Chat,* as the center of frenetic, uncreative activity and a breeding ground for fear and loneliness.

In *Dark Places of the Heart* the emphasis falls differently. The setting is the city once again, in Tyneside and London, but the city seen as the background to Nellie's life and, through the account of the Cotters, to the English working classes and the muddle of their political fortunes. Nellie's brother Tom, endowed with more imagination than is good for his peace of mind, is another of the wanderers and seekers first met with in *Seven Poor Men of Sydney.* One of the achievements of *Dark Places of the Heart* is the authentic atmosphere Christina Stead creates of the industrial north with its dreary suburban streets, its grime, and the pervasive, bronchial-breeding dampness of the air.

The contemporary novelist cannot escape the city; whether he likes it or not, it is the center of twentieth-century life. The modern novel is largely the attempt of the writer to come to terms with it. Baudelaire has been taken again, this time by Peter Quennell, to mark the transition to the new urban civilization:

The background of Baudelaire's development is the background of urban civilization. No writer or artist of the past, accustomed to the agglomeration of hovels, merchants' houses and palaces until recently named a city, could have foretold the development of city-life that has taken place within a hundred years, or would have understood how intense a focus of emotional disturbance the modern city might become.[8]

VII   *The Unique Individual*

Christina Stead's fiction continually reflects this disturbed and disturbing world as a matter of course, but it does not subordinate the individual to society in any simple, determinist way. Even Letty Fox, who is more a victim of society than the other heroines, asserts herself in a struggle against the forces that deny her freedom and fulfilment. The people who are overwhelmed, like Michael and Henny, go under because they will not, cannot, surrender their individuality. The most memorable of Christina Stead's characters, both the attractive and the unattractive, remain stubbornly unique; Raccamond and Léon, Teresa and Crow, Sam and Louisa, Nellie Cotter—whether succeeding or failing they are, as individuals, bigger and more interesting than the environments that have shaped them. For such apparently old-fashioned literary virtues we may still feel grateful in an age which has made a fetish of novelty and experimentation, and which has presented so many "novels" that turn out to be propaganda, confessions, reportage, pornography, tracts for the times, typographical jokes— anything, indeed, but genuine fiction.

Commending Christina Stead as a genuine novelist may also force us to reconsider our priorities. Ours is an age which brings out with monotonous regularity book after book on the select few. The commentaries on Joyce, Lawrence, and Faulkner alone would constitute a sizable library in themselves. In consequence there are numerous critical studies which work over the same ground and come to much the same general conclusions. There are, also, many painstakingly detailed researches into obscure biographical matters and into the sources from which the select few have drawn material for their novels. Must we continue to listen to critics trying to say something new about D. H. Lawrence's philosophy or discovering further allusions and literary parallels in *Ulysses*? How many more books do we need to ferret out the autobiographical elements, as yet unaccounted for, in Conrad's fiction—to identify beyond doubt the real-life figure who gave the novelist the *idea* for the character of Lord Jim? Some of this energy might more profitably be directed elsewhere. After all, there are other twentieth-century novelists worth reading and studying. Christina Stead is one of these.

Notes and References

Chapter One

1. Jean Saxelby and Gwen Walker-Smith, "Christina Stead," *Biblio-news*, Book Collectors' Society of Australia, II (December, 1949), 40.
Uncle Percival Hogg builds his country home on Lydnam Hill and calls it Lydnam Lodge. Nature lover, reformer, and crank, he has something in common with Sam Pollit of *The Man Who Loved Children*. See *Letty Fox*, Chapter IV.

2. French idioms occasionally slip through in *House of All Nations:* for example, p. 152. " 'Where will be all of us in a few years?' "; p. 319. "There is Griffin's, a good restaurant"; and p. 377. " 'You can't tell me he's been with the Lord since fifteen years and got nothing out of it.' "

3. In her autobiography *Child of the Hurricane*, Sydney, Angus and Robertson, 1964, Katharine Susannah Prichard, when describing her journeys overseas as a young woman, says that to establish herself as a writer in Australia she felt she had first to win recognition elsewhere.

4. R. P. Blackmur, "The American Literary Expatriate," in *The Lion and the Honeycomb* (London, 1956), p. 74.

5. Martin Boyd, *Outbreak of Love* (London, 1957), pp. 127–28.

Chapter Two

1. "Christina Stead," *Southerly*, VII, 2 (1946), 87. The source of the information that follows in this paragraph is the author herself. It might also be noted that, in addition to the four stories listed, certain of the others exhibit Australian settings, scenery, and imagery.

2. *Laughter, Not for a Cage* (Sydney, 1956).

3. Even H. M. Green, who praises *Seven Poor Men of Sydney*, is wide of the mark when he generalizes about the main characters: ". . . all are intellectuals, all are unfortunate and defeated persons, and most of them are unhealthy in mind and body." *A History of Australian Literature*, II (Sydney, 1961), 1071. (Hereafter referred to as Green Vol. II.) This remark is quite misleading. The Folliots and Mendelssohn may truly be described as intellectuals; certainly Joseph

and Chamberlain are not. This chapter enters reservations about the remainder of this generalization by Green.

4. *Seven Poor Men of Sydney* (Sydney, 1965), pp. 2–3.

5. See M. Barnard Eldershaw, "Christina Stead" in *Essays in Australian Fiction* (Melbourne, 1938), especially pp. 174–76. (Hereafter referred to as Barnard Eldershaw.)

6. See p. 60 and pp. 11–12, 269–70. See also p. 268, where in describing one of his dehumanizing experiences Michael talks of a woman with "moon-white hair."

7. See too Michael's words: " 'I spoil everything I touch because I was born without hands—like poor Blount, for all practical purposes' " (p. 220).

   But, for another instance of Christina Stead's detachment, see also Mendelssohn on Kol Blount (p. 310).

8. "A Reader's Notebook," *All About Books,* Melbourne, February 11, 1935, p. 22.

9. *Australian Women's Weekly,* March 9, 1935. A report of Christina Stead's comments as communicated to an overseas representative of the paper. The author has endorsed the accuracy of the report.

10. *Times Literary Supplement,* February 15, 1934.

11. *The Fairies Return* or New Tales for Old By Several Hands. With reverent apologies to the memory of Perrault, the Brothers Grimm, Hans Andersen, the authors of The Thousand and One Nights, etc. (London, 1934).

12. *The Salzburg Tales* (London, 1934), p. 498.

13. Green, II, 1172.

14. *Reading I've Liked* (London, 1946), p. 521.

15. Green, II, 1172–73.

16. Barnard Eldershaw, p. 167.

17. Barnard Eldershaw, p. 165.

18. *Reading I've Liked,* p. 521.

19. See the comments of the German Student, *The Salzburg Tales,* p. 199. Since this chapter was written Christina Stead has published another novel, *Dark Places of the Heart,* where the recurring imagery of the mirror confirms the argument put forward here. See Chapter 6, pp. 157–58.

20. Unlike certain Australian critics, the reviewer in the *Times Literary Supplement,* November 8, 1934, was well aware of this artistic detachment. Indeed, he went on to argue that Christina Stead's "cool and ironical impartiality" was insufficient "to quicken the scene into life."

Chapter Three

1. *Australian Women's Weekly,* March 9, 1935.
2. The epithet "Munchausen" first occurs in *Seven Poor Men of Sydney,* p. 161, where it is applied by Joseph to Withers.
3. *The Beauties and Furies* (New York, 1936), p. 95.
4. May 22, 1936.
5. *Southerly,* VII, 2 (1946), 88.
6. Barnard Eldershaw, p. 159.
7. The most favorable opinion I have been able to find of *The Beauties and Furies* is a review by J. G. Conant entitled "The Revolutionary Fringe," *New Masses,* August 4, 1936, pp. 25–26. As his title suggests, Conant sees the book as a study of types "who play around the edges of revolutionary realities." But despite the high praise he gives it, Conant also feels that its true significance is liable to be lost through overelaboration of language.
8. Marpurgo introduces himself to Oliver thus: "'. . . I'm a sort of fabulist, the Arabian Nights is my natural background.'" *The Beauties and Furies,* p. 10. In "The Amenities" occurs a description of the elaborate suite of the wealthy business man Henry Van Laer, followed by this passage: "Let no-one think that this is a ridiculous account of the suite of the once-famous Van Laer, for much more fantastic legends are regularly current about the financial wizards and mystery-men of the Stock Exchange who spring up frequently in the nightmarish financial world." *The Salzburg Tales,* p. 277.
9. *New Masses,* January 20, 1942.
10. For a full account of the complexities of the situation see Alphendéry's explanation to Adam Constant, about to go to England as Jules's emissary in this affair. Pp. 500–2.
11. "The House that Jack Built," *New Masses,* June 21, 1938.
12. For example, *Scene Fifteen* (exploiting inflation); and the whole of the contre-partie business.
13. *The Beauties and Furies,* p. 98.
14. To Alphendéry, Jules is the quicksands and Léon the volcano. See p. 370.
15. See, too, p. 539, where Alphendéry, unlike the others, believes the best of Raccamond, and turns out to be right.
16. *Time* Magazine, June 13, 1938.
17. *Sydney Morning Herald,* July 22, 1938.
18. *Ibid.*
19. The two principal passages analyzing Jules are *Scene Nine* and *Scene Seventy-four.* Is there some contradiction in the author's comments? Cf. "vapid cynicism" (p. 88) with p. 597, where we are

informed that Jules believes nothing that is told him, "not out of cynicism, but out of the clarity of his nature."

20. See for example *Tom Jones*, Book IX, Chapter V; the eating scene at the inn preceding the seduction of Tom by Mrs. Waters. Tony Richardson, the producer of the recent film, *Tom Jones*, gave a rather different emphasis to Fielding's metaphor and developed a brilliant scene in which the pleasures of eating anticipate the erotic delights to follow.

21. See pp. 283–85 for Madame Haller's ambivalent attitude toward Raccamond.

Chapter Four

1. *The Man Who Loved Children* (New York, 1965), p. 443.
2. *Ibid.* Cf. pp. 127–28 with pp. 145, 149, 179.
3. *New York Review*, June 17, 1965.
4. *The Man Who Loved Children*, Introduction, pp xxxii–iii.
5. For example, San Francisco *People's World*, September 4, 1965.
6. Isidor Schneider, *New Masses*, November 12, 1940.
7. *A View of My Own* (London, 1964), p. 45.
8. *Sunday Herald Tribune*, April 18, 1965.
9. *Australian Letters*, November, 1958.
10. Cf. also Mendelssohn's speculations on the possibiliy of Australians becoming, like certain older civilizations, a nation of star-gazers. *Seven Poor Men of Sydney*, p. 314.
11. *The Flesh and the Spirit* (Sydney, 1948), p. 238.
12. The same allusion occurs in *Seven Poor Men of Sydney*, p. 167, where Cytherea (Cythera) suggests the opening up of the world of art to the uninitiated; and again in *The Man Who Loved Children*, p. 436, in a passage of adolescent gush that Louisa writes to her school friend Clare.
13. *The Life of Saint Teresa*, translated by J. M. Cohen (Harmondsworth, 1957), p. 114.
14. "Prelude," I (London, 1948), xv, xvi.
15. *Don Quixote*, translated by Samuel Putnam, Vol. I (London, 1953), Prologue.
16. Louis Untermeyer has an apt description, ". . . the crowded gaiety of the Breughel-like wedding scene." *Modern Women in Love* (New York, 1945), Introduction, p. xvi.

Chapter Five

1. For examples see titles and comments in *Selected Bibliography*. III. *Reviews* 5.
2. *Laughter, Not for a Cage*, p. 180.
3. *Australian Literature* (London, 1960), p. 248.

4. *Letty Fox: Her Luck* (London, 1947), pp. 11–12.

5. New York *Times,* June 9, 1946.

6. "Christina Stead," *Biblionews,* XI (January, 1958), 3.

7. See for example pp. 109, 162–63, 166, 487–88.

8. See for example pp. 60, 77, 81, 105.

9. Pp. 87–88. See, too, paragraph p. 187 on Grandmother Fox.

10. The reviewer for the Sydney *Bulletin,* October 20, 1948, held the basic fault to be "Social Purpose," and found the book difficult "to the point of impossibility."

11. The author herself describes it as a suggestion only, not a direct parallel. "Don Juan in the Arena" (*The Salzburg Tales*) is another version of the legend.

12. The image of Azrael is a recurrent one, to be found in *House of All Nations, The Man Who Loved Children, For Love Alone, Letty Fox, A Little Tea, a Little Chat, The People with the Dogs.*

13. *Nation,* April 5, 1965.

14. See *For Love Alone,* p. 219; *The Man Who Loved Children,* pp. 232, 272, 353; "U.N.O. 1945," *Southerly,* XXII, 4 (1962), 242.

15. Edward says his grandfather "wanted half-way a community like that at Oneida." *The People with the Dogs* (Boston, 1952), p. 88.

Chapter Six

1. *Kenyon Review,* XX VII, 3 (1965), 456.

2. Jose Yglesias, *Nation,* October 24, 1965.

3. *Listener,* December 5, 1934.

4. *New Masses,* January 20, 1942.

5. Quoted in Miriam Allott, *Novelists on the Novel* (London, 1965 Reprint), p. 66.

6. *Ibid.,* p. 68.

7. *The Roaring Twenties* (London, 1960), p. 152.

8. *Baudelaire and the Symbolists* (London, 1954), p. 41.

Selected Bibliography

The Canadian editions, published concurrently with most of the American first editions, have not been listed.

Under *Miscellaneous* I have included only two reviews by Christina Stead, her longest and most interesting—that on Saroyan for its trenchant criticism and that on Aragon for its generalizations about the long modern novel. Under *Reviews* of Christina Stead's fiction I have selected those which, favorable or unfavorable, make some attempt at analysis and understanding. I have also included a few for other reasons—to represent typical attitudes, and critical obtuseness or other kinds of unfairness.

PRIMARY SOURCES

I. Works by Christina Stead

1. *Fiction: First Publications*

The Salzburg Tales. London: Peter Davies, 1934. New York: D. Appleton-Century, 1934.

Seven Poor Men of Sydney. London: Peter Davies, 1934. New York: D. Appleton-Century, 1935.

The Beauties and Furies. London: Peter Davies, 1936. New York: D. Appleton-Century, 1936.

House of All Nations. New York: Simon and Schuster, 1938. London: Peter Davies, 1938.

The Man Who Loved Children. New York: Simon and Schuster, 1940. London: Peter Davies, 1941.

For Love Alone. New York: Harcourt, Brace, 1944. London: Peter Davies, 1945.

Letty Fox: Her Luck. New York: Harcourt, Brace, 1946. London: Peter Davies, 1947.

A Little Tea, a Little Chat. New York: Harcourt, Brace, 1948.

The People with the Dogs. Boston: Little, Brown, 1952.

Dark Places of the Heart. New York: Holt, Rinehart, and Winston, 1966.

[*Cotters' England.*] London: Secker and Warburg, 1967.
The Puzzleheaded Girl. New York: Holt, Rinehart, and Winston, 1967.

2. *Fiction: Reissues.*

The Man Who Loved Children. New York: Holt, Rinehart, and Winston, 1965. London: Secker and Warburg, 1966.
Seven Poor Men of Sydney. Sydney: Angus and Robertson, 1965.
For Love Alone. Sydney: Angus and Robertson, 1966.
The Salzburg Tales. Melbourne: Sun Books, 1966.

3. *Translations* (Of novels)

For Love Alone under title, *Tutto Accade a Chi Vuole.* Milan: Baldini and Castoldi, 1947 (Translator, Chiara Salimei); and under title, *Vent d'Amour.* Paris: Editions des Deux-Rives, 1948 (Translator, Gabriel Beaucé).

4. *Short Stories*

"O, If I Could but Shiver," in *The Fairies Return.* London: Peter Davies, 1934, pp. 289–310.
"The Hotel-keeper's Story" in *Southerly*, XIII, 2 (1952), 74–82.
"A Household" ⎫ in *Southerly*, XXII, 4 (1962),
"U.N.O. 1945" ⎭ 213–34, 235–53.
"The Puzzleheaded Girl" in *Kenyon Review*, XXVII, 3 (1965), 399–456. Also appeared in *Australian Letters*, VII, 2 (1966), 26–62.
"The Huntress" in *Saturday Evening Post*, October 23, 1965.
"The Woman in the Bed" in *Meanjin*, XXVII, 4 (1968), 430–52.

5. *Articles*

"A Writer's Friends" in *Southerly*, XXVIII, 3 (1968), 163–8.
"The International Symposium on the Short Story." Christina Stead (England) in *Kenyon Review*, XXX, 4 (1968), 444–50.

6. *Translations* (By Christina Stead, from the French)

GIGON, FERNAND. *Colour of Asia.* London: Muller, 1955.
GILTÈNE, JEAN. *The Candid Killer.* London: Muller, 1956.
PICCARD, AUGUSTE. *In Balloon and Bathyscaphe.* London: Cassell, 1956.

7. *Anthologies*

STEAD, CHRISTINA and BLAKE, WILLIAM, eds. *Modern Women in Love.* New York: Dryden Press, 1945.
STEAD, CHRISTINA, ed. *Great Stories of the South Sea Islands.* London: Muller, 1955.

8. *Miscellaneous*

"The Writers Take Sides," *Left Review,* August, 1935.

"The Impartial Young Man," review of *Inhale and Exhale* by William Saroyan, *New Masses,* March 17, 1936.

Review of *The Century Was Young* by Louis Aragon, *New Masses,* January 20, 1942.

SECONDARY SOURCES

I. Critical and Biographical

ELDERSHAW, M. BARNARD. "Christina Stead" in *Essays in Australian Fiction.* Melbourne: Melbourne University Press, 1938, pp. 158–81. A good essay but deals with the first three books only.

FADIMAN, CLIFTON. *Reading I've Liked.* London: Hamish Hamilton, 1946, pp. 521–22. A short commentary on *The Salzburg Tales.*

FRANKLIN, MILES. *Laughter, Not for a Cage.* Sydney: Angus and Robertson, 1956, pp. 172–73, 179–80.

GEERING, R. G. "The Achievement of Christina Stead," in *Southerly,* XXII, 4 (1962), 193–212.

———. "Introduction" to *Seven Poor Men of Sydney.* Sydney: Angus and Robertson, 1965, pp. ix–xv.

———. "Christina Stead in the 1960s" in *Southerly,* XXVIII, 1 (1968), 26–36.

GREEN, DOROTHY. "Chaos, on a Dancing Star? Christina Stead's *Seven Poor Men of Sydney*" in *Meanjin,* XXVII, 2 (1968), 150–61.

GREEN, H. M. *A History of Australian Literature.* II, 1923–50. Sydney: Angus and Robertson, 1961, 1070–77, 1172–73.

HADGRAFT, CECIL. *Australian Literature, a Critical Account to 1955.* London: Heinemann, 1960, pp. 246–48. Includes Christina Stead in chapter on "Modern Fiction" under the "psychological novel" but queries her "ability to create characters." Calls *The Salzburg Tales* a novel, and dismisses the later books, including *The Man Who Loved Children.*

HARDWICK, ELIZABETH. "The Neglected Novels of Christina Stead," in *A View of My Own.* London: Heinemann, 1964, pp. 41–48. This essay first appeared as an article in *New Republic,* August 1, 1955. Deals mainly with *The Man Who Loved Children;* calls *The Salzburg Tales* a novel and describes it as "long, stately, impressive and unreadable" and a "strangely gifted failure."

HESELTINE, HARRY. "Australian Fiction Since 1920," in *The Literature of Australia.* Ed. Dutton, Geoffrey. Harmondsworth: Penguin, 1964, p. 187. One paragraph comparing Christina Stead

with Chester Cobb and discussing *Seven Poor Men of Sydney*
only.

HOWARTH, R. G. "Christina Stead," in *Biblionews*. Book Collectors' Society of Australia, XI (January, 1958), 1–3. Deals largely with
The Man Who Loved Children.

JARRELL, RANDALL. "An Unread Book," Introduction to *The Man Who
Loved Children*. New York: Holt, Rinehart, and Winston, 1965,
and London: Secker and Warburg, 1966.

MILLER, E. MORRIS and MACARTNEY, FREDERICK T. *Australian Literature*. Sydney: Angus and Robertson, revised ed. 1956, pp. 440–
42. Bibliographical work which contains useful commentaries.
The comments on Christina Stead reveal some minor errors (in
naming characters). This bibliography lists the English edition
of *House of All Nations* as *The Revolving Hive*. This title was
once considered but the book was published by Peter Davies as
House of All Nations.

RODERICK, COLIN. "Christina Stead," in *Southerly*, VII, 2 (1946),
87–92.

————. *An Introduction to Australian Fiction*. Sydney: Angus and
Robertson, 1950, pp. 132–38.

SAXELBY, JEAN and WALKER-SMITH, GWEN. "Christina Stead," in
Biblionews. Book Collectors' Society of Australia, II (December,
1949), 37–43.

STEWART, DOUGLAS. "Glory and Catastrophe," in *The Flesh and the
Spirit*. Sydney: Angus and Robertson, 1948, pp. 235–38. An essay on *For Love Alone*.

WILDING, MICHAEL. "Christina Stead's Australian Novels," in *Southerly*,
XXVII, 1 (1967), 20–33.

II. Reviews

1. *The Salzburg Tales.*

London *Times*, January 30, 1934.
Times Literary Supplement, February 15, 1934.
Sydney Morning Herald, May 4, 1934.

2. *Seven Poor Men of Sydney.*

London *Times*, November 2, 1934.
Times Literary Supplement, November 8, 1934.
London *Time and Tide*, November 10, 1934. By Ralph Bates; sensi-
tive and balanced.
Sydney *Bulletin*, November 28, 1934.
Listener, December 5, 1934. By Edwin Muir; most perceptive.
Sydney Morning Herald, December 7, 1934.

Canberra *Australian*, March 19, 1966.
Melbourne *Age*, March 26, 1966.
Sydney MorningHerald, June 11, 1966. Very favorable.
Sydney *Nation*, June 11, 1966.

3. *The Beauties and Furies.*

New York *Herald Tribune*, April 26, 1936. A strong attack.
Times Literary Supplement, May 2, 1936. Critical but fair.
New York *Times Book Review*, May 3, 1936.
Sydney Morning Herald, May 22, 1936.
New Masses, August 4, 1936. "The Revolutionary Fringe" by J. G.
   Conant. Controversial and stimulating—in defense.

4. *House of All Nations.*

Times Literary Supplement, June 11, 1938. Severe in places; well
   argued.
Time, June 13, 1938. Most enthusiastic.
New Masses, June 21, 1938. By Edwin Berry Burgum. Emphasizes
   political implications; well-written and stimulating.
Listener, June 30, 1938. By Edwin Muir. Rated well below *Seven
   Poor Men of Sydney.*
Sydney Morning Herald, July 22, 1938.

5. *The Man Who Loved Children.*

New York *Herald Tribune Books*, October 13, 1940. Favorable.
New York *Times*, October 18, 1940. Favorable.
New Yorker, October 19, 1940. By Clifton Fadiman. Very favorable.
New York *Times Book Review*, October 20, 1940. By M. H. Very
   favorable. Notes "curious relationship" between this book and
   Moby Dick.
New Masses, November 12, 1940. Very favorable.
Saturday Review, November 16, 1940. Very favorable.
Times Literary Supplement, July 12, 1941. Dismisses book as a failure.
Sydney Morning Herald, September 20, 1941. Very favorable.
Washington *Sunday Star*, March 7, 1965. Very favorable. Takes up
   Jarrell's *Moby Dick* comparison and develops an elaborate series
   of parallels.
Time, April 2, 1965.
Nation, April 5, 1965. By Jose Yglesias. A long review, plus general
   comment on Christina Stead's work; stresses political elements. A
   valuable analysis.
Saturday Review, April 10, 1965.
New York *Sunday Herald Tribune Book Week*, April 18, 1965. By
   Eleanor Perry. Long and appreciative discussion.

New York Review, June 17, 1965. By Christopher Ricks. First-class analysis, especially good in discussing Christina's Stead's use of language.

San Francisco *People's World,* September 4, 1965. Seen as an exposé of "the inhuman condition of the bourgeoisie."

London *Observer,* May 22, 1966. By John Wain. Rates it as a major novel.

6. *For Love Alone.*

Sydney Morning Herald, December 30, 1944. Favorable.

Sydney *Daily Telegraph,* January 13, 1945. Favorable.

Times Literary Supplement, October 13, 1945. Dismisses book as an utter failure, worse than *The Man Who Loved Children.*

Spectator, October 26, 1945. Pretty severe on Jonathan Crow, but can see other virtues in the book.

Listener, November 1, 1945. By Desmond Hawkins; "an Australian *Sons and Lovers* with a feminine Paul Morel."

Sydney Morning Herald, October 8, 1966. By Barbara Jefferis. Critical and appreciative.

7. *Letty Fox: Her Luck.*

New York *Times,* June 9, 1946. By Mary McGrory. Severe, but intelligent and well argued.

New York *Herald Tribune Weekly Book Review,* October 20, 1946. "Sex Ferment, Home Brewed."

New Masses, December 10, 1946. Unfavorable.

Sydney Morning Herald, March 1, 1947. By K. M. Inaccurate, wild, and bitter attack.

Times Literary Supplement, April 12, 1947. Again *T. L. S.* brands book as a failure.

Sydney *Bulletin,* October 20, 1948. "Red Page" article entitled "Urban and Rustic"; compares *Letty Fox* with a novel (*Tidal Creek*) of New Zealand country life.

8. *A Little Tea, a Little Chat.*

Time, September 13, 1948.

9. *Dark Places of the Heart.*

New York *Herald Tribune Book Week,* September 11, 1966. By Paul West. Appreciative and well written.

Time, September 23, 1966. "It is certainly one of the most peculiar books ever written by a novelist of undoubtedly great talents." Reviewer is a long way behind the novelist; fails to note the most important thing about Nellie.

Nation, October 24, 1966. "Marking off a Chunk of England." Jose Yglesias acclaims it as a masterpiece and Christina Stead as one of the great writers of our time. Very perceptive analysis of the novel and good on generalizations.

III. General

LINDSAY, JACK. *Life Rarely Tells.* London: Bodley Head, 1958. *The Roaring Twenties.* London: Bodley Head, 1960. *Fanfrolico and After.* London: Bodley Head, 1962. Three-volume autobiography; first volume deals mainly with early years in Brisbane, second volume with literary life in Sydney, 1921–26, and third with Lindsay's struggle to establish himself as writer and publisher in London.

————. "Vision of the Twenties," in *Southerly,* XIII, 2 (1952). Tells of his own literary struggles and wants to show "how other writers of my generation, such as Christina Stead, have also developed through a conflict between their Australian basis and their European participations a form of growth which could wholly exist only for our generation, the generation of the complex transitional movement I am here analysing." (p. 68).

STEPHENSEN, P. R. *The Foundations of Culture in Australia.* An Essay towards National Self Respect. Gordon: W. J. Miles, 1936. Stephensen laments the departure of artistic talent to England but undermines his case by remarks such as the following: "There is more poetical sophistication in a page of Brennan, of Baylebridge, of McCrae, or of Jack Lindsay, than in a whole volume of Eliot" (p. 111). "Had these people [talented Australians] remained here, and dealt with the realities of Australia, instead of with the fantasies of European glamour and European antiquity . . ." (p. 123).

Index